W9-BLU-466

arms of the chair and lifted Teddy up. He unfolded a striped sheet. And draped it around my son's neck. Then he cleared his throat and asked, 'What will it be this morning, mister, a shave?' "

—He takes Teddy to a full-scale Gilbreth Nantucket family reunion: "We were met by three automobiles containing seventeen people, two dogs, one cat, and a caged parakeet, which has never talked, perhaps because he never had a fair chance. Teddy went through the motions of shaking hands. Then after he had finally made the rounds, he drawled in his best Charlestonese, 'Gracious God, do we have to shake hands all day? I never shook hands with so many head of people in my bored days.' "

About the Author

FRANK B. GILBRETH has authored or co-authored nine books. He has lived in Charleston, S. C. for many years though originally he came from the North where he was reared in Providence, R. I. and Montclair, N. J. Eldest son of the famous Gilbreth dozen, he was graduated from the University of Michigan and has spent all of his life in newspaper work. He was successively a reporter for the N. Y. *Herald Tribune,* The Associated Press and the Charleston *News and Courier.* During World War II he received the bronze star and air medal as a naval officer in the Pacific. He is now vice-president and assistant publisher of the Charleston, S. C. *News and Courier* and the Charleston *Post.*

HE'S MY BOY

BOOKS BY FRANK B. GILBRETH, JR.

I'M A LUCKY GUY

INNSIDE NANTUCKET

OF WHALES AND WOMEN

HOW TO BE A FATHER

LOBLOLLY

HE'S MY BOY

BY FRANK B. GILBRETH, JR., AND ERNESTINE GILBRETH CAREY

CHEAPER BY THE DOZEN

BELLES ON THEIR TOES

BY FRANK B. GILBRETH, JR., AND JOHN HELD, JR.

HELD'S ANGELS

HE'S MY BOY

BY FRANK B. GILBRETH, JR.

With drawings by Vasiliu

DODD, MEAD & COMPANY

NEW YORK

1962

DISCARDED

SCHENECTADY COUNTY
PUBLIC LIBRARY

COPYRIGHT © 1962 BY FRANK B. GILBRETH, JR.
ALL RIGHTS RESERVED
NO PART OF THIS BOOK MAY BE REPRODUCED IN ANY FORM
WITHOUT PERMISSION IN WRITING FROM THE PUBLISHER
LIBRARY OF CONGRESS CATALOG CARD NUMBER: 62-8751

PRINTED IN THE UNITED STATES OF AMERICA
BY VAIL-BALLOU PRESS, INC., BINGHAMTON, N.Y.

FEB 21 1962

817
G46he
c. 7

TO MARY

CONTENTS

vii

viii   CONTENTS

HE'S MY BOY

CHAPTER 1

BIRTHDAY PARTY

NOT LONG AGO, ON A FRAGRANT SPRING DAY IN CHARLESTON, South Carolina, I had a passive role in my son's fourth birthday party. And although I'm forty-five years older than he, it pleased me to observe that the amenities of such affairs haven't changed a whit since the days when I was a precious Little Lord Fauntleroy in Buster Brown collar and flowing red tie.

The birthday parties are still bedlam, of course—a high-pitched and generally masochistic bit of trauma for all hands and the cook. But they serve a useful purpose, particularly

1

for believers in the American dream.

Because if a boy is going to be a success in life, you can't start tutoring him too soon on how to be a money-making extrovert who enjoys the limelight. Birthday parties teach him how to preside over meetings, and how to play the part of Good Fellow while extracting booty from his peers.

With proper training along such lines, there is no telling what heights the boy might reach in business and especially in politics.

And while it would certainly be tempting the fates to start teaching him to recognize such melodies as "Happy Days Are Here Again" and "Hail to the Chief," still *somebody* has to be ready to take over certain man-killing duties, in the event of a mandate from the voters.

In Charleston, children are brought to soirees by colored nurses, who all pitch in and help serve the food, and then have a soiree of their own in the kitchen.

Except for these colored nurses—and of course the nature of the presents—my son's birthday party was exactly like the ones we used to have where I grew up, in Providence, Rhode Island.

So I could almost turn back the clock to my own boyhood, just before World War I, when the *bon mot* of the day—"It's naughty but it's nice"—expressed the whole racy renaissance of a new jazz-age generation intent on scrapping the last traces of Victorianism. In those days, there were still as many horses as automobiles in the streets of Providence, and it was just becoming fashionable to convert house lights from gas to electricity.

It's true that at birthday parties today, space ships, disintegrator guns, artificial satellites, and skin-diving equipment have largely replaced the jackstraws, parcheesi sets, authors' cards, and kaleidoscopes of my time.

But the point is that the trappings and etiquette of the parties haven't changed.

The scrubbed little guests, who aren't at all sure they should have come in the first place, still require considerable prodding before they will yield their presents to the honoree. And the honoree himself at first views the gifts with suspicion. He's hazy as to why certain acquaintances who usually greet him with a shove, a cuff, or a kick are now showering him so generously with largess.

But as soon as it becomes plain to him that the gifts are, in fact, his tribute, the Birthday Boy becomes intolerably grasping. He greets his guests greedily with outstretched hands, demanding:

"Hey, you! Give me my present!"

"You mustn't act like *that!*" his mother chides him. "That's no way for a host to treat his guests."

"Well it's my birthday, and they're *supposed* to bring birthday presents whenever I have a birthday," he points out all too logically.

Each guest watches intently and expectantly as the gift he has brought is torn open by the Birthday Boy. But if the guest expects to be overwhelmed with gracious thanks, he's in for a rude disappointment. For the most part, Birthday Boy stands mute and doesn't even change his expression, as he extracts the loot from its tissue-paper covering.

To make up for Birthday Boy's bad manners his mother finds herself becoming more and more effusive. "Oh, what a perfectly lovely little death-ray gun," she babbles. "My goodness, isn't it a real beauty? It was *so* thoughtful of you, dear, to bring it. A cute, little death-ray gun! There's not a single one in the house, either, so we certainly did need it."

As the bounty piles up, Birthday Boy becomes more and more sated with his own opulence. Then he puts some presents aside without deigning to open them, and gives short shrift to the ones his mother opens for him.

As at the annual weighing of the Aga Khan, the pile of presents soon duplicates the displacement of Birthday Boy himself. But by now he is thoroughly bored, and he couldn't care less.

"Gracious, what a perfectly lovely little first-aid kit," the mother continues to enthuse desperately. "And *look!* Here's a bottle of make-believe tranquilizer pills. It was so thoughtful of you dear, and I want you to be *sure* to tell your mother that it's just exactly what we needed."

She sounds as if she wishes the tranquilizers were the real thing.

Luckily, at this point in the procedure, refreshments are served, and the guests fight their way into the dining room, except for the shy ones who slowly bring up the rear, and the really shy ones who are dragged.

The table-setting hasn't changed a bit since my time. At each place—in addition to two plates, silver, and a paper napkin—are the following items:

—A white paper cup filled with green, white, and pink peppermints.

—A crepe-paper-covered "popper" which makes a bang like a cap-pistol when you pull it apart, and which subsequently disgorges a paper hat and a little trinket.

—A horn, deliberately designed to add a touch of wild cacophony to the existing bedlam.

—A tightly coiled paper object which, when blown into, suddenly unrolls into a quivering snake.

—A ribbon, which leads to a grab bag in the center of the table. At a signal from Birthday Boy's mother, each child will pull his ribbon, and a present will emerge. Although Birthday Boy has grown bored with his *own* presents, he has now become so self-important that it's difficult to convince him the grab bag presents aren't all meant for him, too.

The standard menu is still fruit punch, cookies, nuts, and ice cream—with the ice cream often molded into such objects as footballs for the boys, and dolls or flowers for the girls.

And then, while the honoree's mother tries to whip up some enthusiasm for the group-singing of "Happy Birthday to You," the cake is triumphantly trotted forward, with four candles ablaze.

This pièce de résistance is the climax of the gala affair. From experience garnered at previous soirees—both his own and his friends'—Birthday Boy knows exactly what is expected of him.

Experimentally, like an athlete preparing to give his all, he takes two or three big, sighing breaths, getting himself limbered up by sucking in his stomach and extending his chest bellows-fashion. Then, exhaling until he's nothing but a round-shouldered, hollow-cheeked shell, he slowly inhales a gigantic chestful.

At this moment-of-truth, an expectant lull descends over the table. All eyes are focused on the four candles. The honoree, his own eyes and cheeks popping from the pressure stored within, leans forward. His face is tense and brick red.

Suddenly, with a misty exhalation, he sprays the cake and the children closest to him with an unhygienic blast. No sperm whale, breaching triumphantly after a mile-deep dive, ever blew more enthusiastically.

The candles sizzle damply, flicker, and give up the ghost. The guests, squealing with excitement, dry their faces with their napkins. Panting from his heroic efforts, Birthday Boy surveys his company with triumph.

And it was at this point that *my* Birthday Boy—his name is Teddy—looked around behind him to make sure that I had witnessed his achievement. For some silly reason, I had been waiting and hoping for him to do just that. A middle-aged father gets mighty wrapped up in his son; maybe too wrapped up, at times, for the good of either himself or his son.

"Did you see that, Daddy?" Teddy crowed. "Were you watching me?"

I told him I hadn't missed a single bit of it.

"I think I done pretty fine," he hollered none too modestly. "I think I done *excellent*. Right?"

"You're darned tooting," I replied, and I hoped no one would notice how pleased I was that, even in the midst of all the excitement, he hadn't forgot to share his triumph with me. "You're batting a thousand, pal."

"Did you see those old candles wave their fire at me, and then go out?"

"I surely did."

"I *certainly* blew out every one of them."

"You certainly did."

"Then are you *proud* of me, Daddy?" he asked, as if the question were all-important.

I told him I was mighty proud of him. Mighty proud indeed.

Teddy's mother came forward, then, with a dull knife. She guided his hand while he hacked out the first piece of birthday cake.

So Teddy was going-on-five. Happy birthday, dear Teddy; happy birthday to you.

I continued to observe the festivities—if that's the word I want—from a distance deemed reasonably safe from spattered or hurled confectioneries. And I felt a stupid lump in my throat.

The world's in a hell of a fix nowadays, what with all the big bombs, and everybody everywhere looking out for No. 1. It's a raw deal—what we used to call hard lines—for Teddy's generation.

And then I thought that, once a man reaches middle age, he can't afford to be cynical. Cynicism is a false face for young fellows who want to hide their disappointment in themselves. It's an I-don't-care mask—an *ish kibibble*.

As everyone knows, though, if you wear your *ish kibibble* too long, you begin to look just like it. And then you cease to be yourself, because even when you take off the mask, you've still got it on.

Certainly a middle-aged man can't afford to be cynical about things which remain as reassuringly constant as children's birthday parties. Anyway, the parties aren't *really* training grounds for money-grubbing extroverts or for political leaders of the future super-states.

In fact, I figure that as long as there are shy, bright-eyed, self-centered little creatures to pipe "Happy Birthday to You," in reedy sopranos, there's still a chance that everything will come out all right after all.

CHAPTER 2

PANCHO AND BOBO

DURING THE YEAR THAT HE'S FOUR YEARS OLD, A BOY emerges from the cocoon of babyhood, and for the first time begins to act and even look like the man he will become. Now he starts to love, hate, reason, scheme, and remember.

This emergence has always been a bittersweet experience for the father to watch. For with the development of guile, which all of God's children must have in order to survive, some of the child's innocence begins to evaporate.

The things that a person remembers first, he also may remember best. And when he's an old man, he may recall snatches of his childhood even more vividly than yesterday.

My most graphic early recollection involves Pancho Villa, the Mexican bandit. Luckily, I never came within a couple of thousand miles of him, which was plenty close enough for me. But he struck terror in my heart, just the same, and I know that as long as I can remember anything, I'll remember him.

I could be fuzzy on a few of the details, because it's hard to separate what you *really* recollect from what you've subsequently been told. But I am positive I recall my father reading aloud from a newspaper about Pancho's sanguinary raids.

I was four or five years old, at the time. And I was sitting with the rest of my family at the battered, oval, mahogany dinner table in the house which we rented for a few years at 77 Brown Street in Providence. It was just one block from the Brown campus where my mother was currently taking her Ph.D. in psychology.

I had on velvet shorts, black-ribbed stockings, and button-shoes, in addition to the Buster Brown collar and flowing red tie that I mentioned before.

My father liked to pontificate at the dinner table, and one of his favorite subjects was current events. How else, he reasoned, could the pre-school illiterates in the family keep abreast of such intelligence as the fact that Langmuir had invented the electron tube multigrid? Or that Little Bill Johnston had given his lumps to McLoughlin in straight sets? Or that Charles Evans Hughes had had the acumen to call President Wilson a dishrag; Jess Willard had thrashed Jack Johnson; Kaiser Bill had twisted the Lion's tail; and Krazy Kat had lost *his* tail in a buzzsaw.

On this particular occasion, my father read us a newspaper article describing all-too-graphically how Villa and his bandits had galloped from Mexico to the United States, and were robbing, ravishing, and bloody-murdering sundry American citizens, especially women and children.

"Hughes is right," my father said darkly. "What else can you expect, with Old Dishrag Wilson in the White House? I tell you, it's going to be a race to see whether the Kaiser or Pancho Villa gets to Washington first. And I'll bet my hat that Old Dishrag spreads a red carpet for whoever wins the race."

I'm sure that this last was deliberately designed to get a rise out of my more moderate mother, who dutifully rose to the bait.

"You're not being fair to the President," she said. "After all, poor Mr. Wilson *has* kept us out of war."

"Ye Gads! Isn't there *any* other thing that *anybody* can say for him?"

"Certainly there is," said my mother, mulling it over. "I'm sure he *means* well."

"So," replied my father, dismissing the argument with one of his favorite comparisons, "does Happy Hooligan!"

I had only the vaguest idea of where Mexico was. And I didn't know what was involved in a ravish, either, although I didn't like the sound of it, and my father had said it was a fate worse than death. But I *did* know that Villa was killing American children, and that I was one of those.

Also, I took quite literally my father's word that if I was depending on Mr. Wilson to stand between me and the scourge of the Rio Grande, I was leaning on a mighty weak dishrag.

I had trouble going to sleep that night, just thinking about it. When I finally went to sleep, I didn't dream. But for some reason, I awoke after midnight, when the house was still, and I was positive that Villa was right there in my room!

I was too terrified to shout, and besides that would only serve to spur Villa to immediate action. I felt the hair rising on my neck, and the chords tighten in my throat. Yes, he had come in the open window, and he was crouched by my bed. He had some kind of a sword in his hand, and in a second he was going to let out a blood-curdling shriek, and run me through.

There was only one thing to do, if I didn't want my number to come up: get the hell out of there. With an economy of motions that would have pleased my efficiency-expert parents, I threw off the covers, streaked into their room, and dived into my father's large brass bed.

"Ye Gads!" he groaned sleepily. "Now who is it *this* time?"

"Me," I admitted.

"Who's me?" he asked, still half asleep. "In this house, you have to be more specific."

"I'm Frank. There's a *man* in my room, Daddy."

That woke him up, not because of the imaginary man, but because he knew this was my first experience of the kind, and he realized how badly frightened I was. He put an arm around me, and idly scratched my back.

"Everything's all right," he reassured me. "You settle down for a minute, and then you can go back to your own bed. There's not *really* any man in there."

"Yes there is," I said. "Pancho Villa's in there. And he has a great big knife."

"Villa!" he repeated, loud enough to wake my mother. "Why Villa's two thousand miles away from here, Franko. Didn't I make that clear? I'm sorry!"

"Which one is it?" Mother asked.

"It's Franko," he told her.

"What is it, dear?" she asked me. "Did you have a nightmare?"

"Not exactly," I explained. "Pancho Villa's in my room, and I'm ascared he's going to ravish me."

They giggled, and my father ran his hand over my ribs, and pinched one of my shoulder blades.

"Quit that," I protested. I giggled, too, but I was still frightened.

"Villa's two thousand miles away," my father repeated. "Besides, boy, you'd make a mighty stingy ravish, even for a Mexican bandit. Now let's all go to sleep. I'm dead tired."

"Can I spend the night in your bed?" I asked.

"Just this once," he agreed. "After that, you'll have to learn not to be afraid of things that don't exist. The trouble is, Franko"—and now he was talking for my mother's benefit again—"if I let one of you children in my bed, I'd have to let *all* of you in. And while a man with seven children forfeits most of his rights, he *does* have the right to sleep in a bed—not a crowded slum or, worse still, a swimming pool."

"Swimming pool!" my mother reproved him. "Shame on you! I don't like jokes like that."

All of that was some forty-five years ago, and it has been at least thirty years since I associated myself with the red-haired, bony, solemn little boy in velvet pants, who grew up in a large, affectionate, and occasionally raucous family.

During most of those years, the little boy didn't exist at all, since I never bothered to think about him. And for awhile, there, his chances of coming back upon the scene were exceedingly slim.

Then I—a widower and father of a splendid grown daughter—married again, and Teddy was born. Teddy doesn't particularly resemble me as a boy, and his temperament is a good deal different. Just the same, he brought that other child back to life. Maybe that's part of what is meant by immortality.

In any event, I'm convinced that the best time of life to be a father of a boy is when a man himself is middle-aged. Old men are apt to hold their sons in awe, and young men to take them for granted. The old father is too far removed from his boyhood to flavor its nostalgia, and the young father is too close.

But fatherhood at middle age—when the days may be dwindling down, but not yet, one fervently hopes, to a precious few—is a delightful baedeker of a man's own boyhood, a guidepost of what songwriters used to persist in calling Memory Lane. It is opportunity's second knock. It is a mirror of one's own tarnished innocence.

I thought of all of that—and particularly of Pancho Villa—shortly after Teddy's fourth birthday. It was early summer in Charleston, then, and the oleanders and crape myrtles were in full bloom. Also, Mary and I were expecting another baby—which I'll get to later.

Among the presents Teddy had received for his birthday—from an aunt and uncle in Birmingham, Alabama—was a roly-poly clown labeled Bo-Bo. The clown was as tall as a man, and had a red, balloon-like nose that whistled satisfyingly when you punched it.

Bo-Bo turned out to be Teddy's favorite gift. He carried the clown from room to room, feeding it, washing its face, socking it until it whistled, and kicking, wrestling, and butt-ing it. Teddy didn't have any playmates who lived near us, so the make-believe clown helped fill the gap.

"Oh, Bo-Bo, you make me laugh all day," the boy would chortle delightedly as the man-sized roly-poly, still smiling stupidly, came bobbing back for more affection or abuse.

And so the two became inseparable. I noticed, though, that Teddy seemed to grow tired of Bo-Bo at bedtime. Twice Teddy locked the clown outside the front door. I found Bo-Bo once under my bed, once under the dining room table, and once in Coventry in the downstairs lavatory where, incidentally, the clown evoked an embarrassed apology from a badly shaken female guest, who was fum-bling for the light switch.

As my father before me, I hold self-evident and am dedi-cated to the proposition that all children are created un-equal to their parents. My father managed to run a fairly taut ship, despite a dozen children. My ship is considerably less taut—sometimes downright slack. Even so, I like to make the rules around my house, and one of the rules is that my son has to pick up his toys.

He obviously wasn't toeing the mark when it came to Bo-Bo, so I set about to correct the situation.

"Teddy, do you know what?" I asked him—and this is the standard maneuver I utilize to capture his attention, when I want to lecture him.

"Yes," he nodded eagerly, perhaps expecting a welcome

surprise.

"Whenever you are through playing with Bo-Bo," I ordered firmly, "I want you to put him in your room. There's a place for everything, and that's his place. I don't want to find him all over the house, after this."

"Not in my room at nighttime, though," said Teddy. "Certainly not."

"*Especially* at nighttime," I corrected him, wanting to avoid any repetition of the debacle in the lavatory. "Put him in your room every night."

"No, certainly not at nighttime," Teddy agreed with himself.

"Why not?"

"Bo-Bo doesn't *like* it there at night."

"Oh, come on, snap out of it, man!" I gave the old fight talk. "Of course he likes it there."

"No he don't."

"I say he does."

"And I say he don't. He told me so, right in my face."

"Why, Teddy," I tried to shame him, "you know he didn't tell you any such thing."

"He did too," the boy contradicted me positively. "He said he *hates* it."

"By granny," I hollered, beginning to lose patience, but still remembering that I mustn't set a bad example by swearing, "let him hate it, then. After this, hate it or not, Bo-Bo spends the night in your room."

"We'll see," Teddy temporized placidly—and for some reason, that suave move to finesse my firm instructions annoyed me even more than open defiance.

"Blast it all and by the great horn spoon! We've already seen! And after this, Bo-Bo spends the night in your room."

"Why you want to holler at me all day?" Teddy inquired. He didn't sound rude, but merely as if his feelings had been hurt, and he was asking the question for information.

"I'm sorry," I apologised. "It's just that sometimes, when you won't listen to what I tell you, you make me mad as a wet hen."

"I listened close," he said with injured innocence.

"Maybe so. But then you said, 'We'll see.' "

"Oh," he nodded non-committally.

That night, we saw: Bo-Bo was hidden under my bed again.

Exasperated, I fished out the clown, kneed him in the groin, and sank my toonder-and-lightning right into his bloated belly. Then I toted him into Teddy's room, and set him down in the middle of the floor.

I was almost mad enough to wake up the boy and lecture him on obedience, because I felt pretty strongly that if I lost this particular battle I'd lose them all—and then he'd be skipper of the ship, instead of me. But he looked so small and unguarded—a little, lone figure in the middle of his crib—that I didn't have the heart. Also, waking Teddy from a sound sleep, for whatever reason, is tempting fate. Both

Mary and I have long since learned to avoid it at all costs, even if we must confiscate the shoes and tape the mouths of boisterous guests.

So I decided to let him sleep. But I made a mental note, when I went to bed, that he and I would have a thorough discussion in the morning about the unwisdom—nay, the sheer folly!—of flagrantly defying my specific commands.

The discussion never took place, though, because around four o'clock that morning I heard my bedroom door open, and Teddy came padding in. He wears the kind of pajamas that have feet as part of the pants, like leotards, so he didn't make much noise. But since it was the first time he had ever roamed around solo like that, I came wide awake in a hurry. I lay still and didn't say anything, because if he were sleep-walking I didn't want to scare him.

I felt him get into my bed and snuggle up against my back, and he was shivering. Remember, it was summertime, too.

"What's the matter, Boy Friend," I finally whispered. It's a term of endearment left over from when he was younger, that I now try to use sparingly. Occasionally it still pops out.

"Bo-Bo," he chattered. "He's in my room."

"Of course he is," I reassured him. "It's all right."

"He must have walked in there."

"No he didn't. Relax. I put him in there."

"But Bo-Bo doesn't *like* it in there."

"Sure he does. He doesn't care where he is. He's just a toy—a clown."

"He's a toy in the daytime," Teddy conceded. "He *certainly* is a toy in the daytime."

"What is he at night, then?"

"What?" he shuddered.

"You know as well as I do."

"What? You tell me."

"He's *still* a clown at night."

"Maybe not, though," gasped Teddy, still shuddering.

"A big fellow like you isn't scared of Bo-Bo!" I said, with a hollow laugh.

"Heck, no," he lied, matching my laugh with an even hollower one.

"No boy of mine is going to be a fraidy-cat, is he?"

"Heck, no."

"I should double-darned well say not," I agreed relying again on the sort of round oaths that fathers reserve especially for their young sons. "My gracious, goodness sake!"

"Who's afraid of a toy clown, eh Daddy?"

"Exactly! Mercy me and heavens alive! That would be ridiculous, wouldn't it?"

"I'll say," Teddy agreed.

"It wouldn't make sense at all, would it?"

"Heck, no. Bo-Bo don't scare *you* at night, does he Daddy!"

"Heck, no," I echoed.

"Good," said Teddy. "Let's bring him in *your* room then. He don't *like* it in my room."

"You mean you don't like to have him there," I accused him. "You're *afraid* of him."

"Not much, though," Teddy defended himself.

"And I thought you told me that Bo-Bo makes you laugh all day."

"All day," he explained. "Not all night, though. It get's dark as a wet hen in my room at night, you know."

"The dark won't hurt you."

"The dark's *good* for you," he said—but he didn't sound as if he meant it. "Can I stay in your bed until morning time, Daddy?"

"I guess so," I agreed. And that was when I started to think about myself as a little boy, and about Pancho Villa. So I reached over and pinched one of Teddy's shoulder blades, as my father used to do mine.

"You *quit* that," he protested happily.

On skinny little boys, those shoulder blades feel almost like wings. Not that there is anything the least bit angelic about the little creatures, though. Usually, quite the contary.

"Will you keep Bo-Bo out of my room at night?"

"All right," I surrendered. "Let's go to sleep."

"Can Bo-Bo sleep in your bed, too?"

"No," I replied firmly. "I draw the line at Bo-Bo. Sorry."

"Does Bo-Bo *scare* you in bed, Daddy?" he asked suspiciously.

"No. I just don't want any big clowns in my bed, that's all."

"Can Bo-Bo sleep *under* your bed?" he persisted.

"I guess so," I conceded sleepily. I was getting mighty tired of the whole subject. "Come on, now. Hush up."

"Or downstairs in the bathroom?"

"I guess so," I surrendered again.

"Bo-Bo *likes* it there," said Teddy. "My gracious, goodness, mercy yes, eh Dad? By granny, eh Dad?"

CHAPTER 3

NEXT GENTLEMAN

MARY AND I WERE CONCERNED THAT SUMMER ABOUT HOW to tell Teddy a new baby was on the way. Since he was a rather dedicated monopolist, we were pretty sure he'd be upset by the thought of competition. Consequently, we wanted to be tactful.

Teddy's never been really spoiled. But the point is that he *was* accustomed to a good deal of attention. And I must admit that he liked his attention to be undivided.

Certainly he had a large and enthusiastic claque: Mary

and me, his nurse, and Mary's parents, who also live in Charleston. And whereas my own mother now has twenty-nine grandchildren, Teddy was the first on Mary's side.

Anyway, Mary and I decided we had better prepare a proper groundwork, before we actually broke the news. We wanted Teddy to be the first to know, and we wanted him to hear it from us. So we kept the news secret from everybody, while we tried to get him accustomed to the idea.

But every time I'd try to brainwash him so that he'd be ready for our news, he'd counter with some propaganda of his own.

"Man, it surely is lonesome around here, don't you think?" I'd ask him. "I wish we had a little baby to play with, don't you?"

"Or a cat," he'd say. "A pussycat would be pretty nice, eh Dad?"

"When I was your age," I told him on another occasion, "I had *lots* of brothers and sisters. And, boy, did we have fun!"

"You did?" he asked eagerly, and I thought that at last I was on the right track. "And did you have lots of pussycats, Dad?"

"If you have a nice, cute baby in the house," I pointed out, "you don't need a cat. Right?"

"Maybe," he agreed. "And if you have a nice pussycat in the house, you don't need a . . ."

"Never mind! How would you like," I dangled a tentative

compromise, "a cute little baby *and* a cat?"

"I want a cat right now," he agreed eagerly.

"What about the new baby?" I asked, insisting on the pound of flesh.

"Okay with me," he nodded with good-humored graciousness.

Since that seemed the apt time to break the news, I pursued the subject further.

"You'll enjoy having a little baby in the house, won't you?" I inquired.

"Yes," he agreed unenthusiastically.

"Won't it be nice to have a little brother or sister to play with?"

"Yes."

"Will you be good to the baby?"

"I guess so."

"And will you let the baby play with your toys?"

"Maybe."

"It's all decided, then, isn't it, Mama?" I asked Mary for his benefit. "We're going to have a new baby pretty soon, and the baby will be Teddy's brother or sister. Won't that be wonderful? And what shall we *name* the new . . ."

"Why," interrupted Teddy firmly but not too impolitely, "do you have to talk all day about babies? Mercy sake!"

Mary tittered, but I was annoyed. Here I had tackled single-handedly the difficult business of breaking the news —and the thanks I got were a giggle from my wife and a sassy brushoff from my son.

"It's no laughing matter," I protested. "I just wanted to be sure that everyone around here understands we're going to have a new baby."

"You don't have to worry about me," said Mary. "I understand, all right."

"Okay, wise guy," I said turning to Teddy. "How about you? Do you understand?"

"We're going to have a new baby *and* a cat," he pointed out.

"All right," I agreed.

"Let's go get the pussycat right now."

"No cat until the baby comes," I insisted.

"Well let's go get the *baby*, then," he suggested. And you couldn't tell whether he wanted the baby, or considered the poor unborn little thing a mere device to get the cat.

"No," replied Mary, "we'll have to wait quite some time for the baby."

"Why?"

"Because it takes time to make babies."

Teddy seemed disappointed. "Darn it," he said. "I wish it was time for the baby to come home right now, don't you, Mama?"

"Yes!" Mary agreed, and the word sounded as if it came from the bottom of her heart. But we still had seven months to wait for that event. And, we still didn't know whether Teddy had actually got the word.

"In the meantime," I promised, "I'll line things up about getting a cat."

"Good boy, Daddy," said Ted.

"Don't give me all the credit," I advised. "Your mother will be busy, too, you know."

"That's about the usual distribution of duties around here," Mary remarked coolly. "I'll have the baby, and your father will find a cat."

"It's the least I can do," I assured her.

Teddy not only *got* the word about the new baby; he wasted no time spreading it. We had intended again to exercise tact, in breaking the news to the domestic help, because a new baby would certainly mean more work. But our young Winchell upset the apple-cart a few days later, at a place called Felder's Palace Barber Shop, where he scooped us in a voice loud enough to be heard not only by Mr. and Mrs. North and South America, but also by quite a few of the ships at sea.

"My daddy and mama are going to bring home a new baby," he broadcast to his barber at a volume just a few decibels below ear-splitting. "What in the world do you think of *that?*"

"You don't say," the barber had the good manners to reply non-committally, without changing his expression. "Now sit still, Teddy-boy, or I might accidentally nick your ear."

That meant the news was out, though, because the barber lives just two houses from Teddy's nurse, across Rutledge Avenue from the Hampton Park Zoo. And also, as always, Felder's was fairly full of patrons, most of whom I knew pretty well. They offered me congratulations, and said that I was a sly old dog—which, for some reason, was exactly what I felt like. Usually I enjoy sitting around Felder's, but occasionally there are drawbacks in going to the same place too often, or even living in the same town too long.

Felder's is owned and run by a group of very light-skinned Negro barbers. They and their predecessors have been catering to "downtown" Charlestonians—the old families—for three generations. The shop is on King Street, in the middle of the retail district, so of course it is patronized by some "uptowners" and some tourists, too, but they're in the minority.

All in all, Felder's is the most prosperous tonsorial parlor in South Carolina—so much so that you have to take a number off a hook, when you enter, to keep track of your turn. Certainly there is some cachet in having a Felder's haircut, and being known, headwaiter-fashion, by the six barbers.

Teddy has been patronizing the shop ever since he was three, and always prefers to wait for his regular barber, who gave him his very first haircut. That first haircut took place at our house, when the boy was about eighteen months old. It was a much-needed and long-overdue amputation of frowsy ringlets, which triggered a severe case of vapors for both Mary and the nurse. Only the barber, Teddy, and I unanimously approved of the results. And having been through that experience together, the three of us have shared a certain camaraderie ever since.

Teddy also shows a precocious interest in the scantily garbed hula dancers which are tatooed on his barber's forearms, and which move cleverly, in a salacious rhythm, when the barber uses a pair of scissors.

Actually, Teddy has had only one haircut at a shop other than Felder's. And that was at Nantucket, Massachusetts, where I took him for a brief vacation, late that same summer, when he was four years old. I'm getting a little ahead of my story, here, but since I'm on the subject of haircuts, I may as well bring in the Nantucket one.

Although Teddy knows and likes all of the easy-going men at Felder's, he was immediately suspicious of the toothy, professionally hearty tonsorial artist who was clipping the summer trade at Nantucket. Frankly, Teddy lacks confidence in white-men-in-white. And while he was perfectly willing to concede that no Nantucket barber had *yet* jabbed him in the rear with a hypodermic needle or tried to grind his teeth with a drill, he was also well aware that there had to be a first time for everything.

"Next gentleman," said the Nantucket barber, and I nudged Teddy forward. He went obediently, but a good deal less than eagerly.

"Well, well," the barber boomed a little too heartily, "what have we got here?"

Ask a stupid question, etc. "A boy," Teddy told him.

"A *boy!*" enthused the barber, as if that was a real eye-opener, and he had been expecting Pithecanthropus Erectus or Yellow Dog Dingo. "What's your name, son?"

"Teddy," he whispered, turning his head away and resting his chin on his right shoulder.

"What? Speak up, son. You don't need to be afraid of me."

"Teddy," he replied, still whispering.

"Freddy!" yelped the barber, who was trying hard to impress everyone in the shop with his ability to handle children. "That's a nice name. And what a coincidence! I have a nephew just about your age, and his name is Freddy, too. What do you think of that?"

If Teddy thought anything of it, he deemed it prudent to reserve judgment and stand mute.

"Teddy," I corrected the barber. "His name's Teddy."

"Oh. Well, Teddy's a nice name, too. Sit right up here, mister."

The barber put a little perch on top of the arms of his chair, and lifted Teddy up. He unfolded a striped sheet, shook it out, and draped in around my son's neck. He worked a foot pedal that raised the chair a little higher. Teddy looked vacantly but self-consciously at me and some other men who were waiting their turn. I knew, and I guess the other men did too, what the barber was going to do next. He was going to pose the exact same question that barbers have been posing of young customers for years.

The barber cleared his throat, and posed it.

"What will it be this morning, mister, a shave?"

"A haircut," Teddy told him patiently.

"No shave, sir?"

"No thank you." He twisted his head, hoping to loosen the striped sheet around his neck. No luck, though.

The barber leaned over him with the clippers. And once again I remembered the prickly sensation clippers used to give me when I was a boy—cold, creepy, and tickly. The barbershops in those days had stuffed owls and mooseheads on the walls, and racks of shaving cups. The barbers chewed tobacco, and colored boys were forever shining the spittoons.

Teddy cringed a bit at the first touch of the clippers, and then hunched his shoulders and grinned sheepishly.

"She won't scare," he assured himself. Translated, that means he was hopeful the clippers—now manipulated by alien hands—would not frighten him into making any sort of craven display.

After awhile, the sheet was removed and shaken again, this time to rid it of the boy's loose hair. Teddy swallowed and moved his neck from side to side, relishing the freedom from the choking pressure. He started to climb out of the chair, but the barber said they weren't quite through.

The sheet was put back again, but this time loosely. Then

came that unforgettable cloud of sweet-smelling powder, dusted liberally from a soft, long-haired brush.

After a few more snips, the barber reached for the comb and brush. Remembering some of the evil and greasy "tonics" of my youth, when we wore our hair parted in the middle and plastered flat, I asked the barber to comb it dry.

He nodded, picked up a straight razor, and stropped it. He squirted a handful of lather from a dispenser, and applied it to Teddy's temples and neck. Carefully, then, he applied the razor. The boy was a study of nonchalance; he didn't move a muscle.

The barber brought out a towel and dried the sideburns and the little neck. Then, with a final flourish he swept off the sheet.

This time the job was really finished, and the boy sighed with relief as he leaped from the chair. I knew his shoulders and back would be itching a little from stray pieces of hair, but that he'd be rather proud of the way he'd behaved. I was too.

"See you around, Freddy," said the barber.

"It's not Freddy, it's Teddy," Teddy corrected him, now facing the man squarely.

"Oh, yeah, that's right! Teddy. See you around, Teddy."

"See you around, White Barber."

"Next gentleman."

CHAPTER 4

DRY HANDS

I'VE BEEN GOING TO NANTUCKET IN THE SUMMERS EVER since I was five or six years old. My mother and two of my brothers have cottages there, and a continuous family reunion, with a varying cast of participants, extends from mid-June to Labor Day.

If it hadn't been for the expected arrival of the new baby, I probably couldn't have talked Mary into letting me take Teddy to Nantucket that summer. But both she and I agreed that what he needed, to prepare him for a baby brother or sister, was to serve a stint in the bosom of a large, noisy, uninhibited, and easy-going family.

My brothers and sisters and assorted children converge on the island from various parts of the country, as their vacation schedules permit. The children, all first cousins, are lumped pretty much into one gregarious tribe. Then the feeding, clothing, and supervision of these Indians—which includes preventing them from drowning, scalping each other, and pulling down the teepees—become a communal responsibility.

All of the cousins are from comparatively small families, and live comparatively staid lives during the rest of the year, so they look forward to their boisterous vacations.

This annual get-together has more appeal, I dare say, for my brothers and sisters than for their spouses. At any rate, that seems to be true of *some* of the spouses, who assert that they are willing—nay, downright eager—to spend their vacations with the members of my family one-at-a-time, or even in small, intimate groups of ten or twelve. But not en masse.

I've never been able to get Mary to say whether or not she'd like to attend a Nantucket reunion. So far, she's never been to one—but there's always *next* year. And, after all, *somebody* has to stay home to guard against a possible invasion by seven-year locusts. Besides, who's going to wind the hall clock and see to it that there's plenty of nice fresh water in the birdbath?

I'll admit, though, that the anticipated Little Stranger constituted a rock-ribbed alibi for Mary's staying away from Nantucket that particular summer. Also, she had a pretty good hunch that this was the year the century plant was going to bloom. And goodness knows she didn't want to miss *that!*

For my part, I looked forward to a first-rate reunion. Even my mother, who is now in her eighties but remains approximately as peripatetic as the late John Foster Dulles, had promised to arrange her schedule so she would be in Nantucket for at least part of the time we were there. I had written her in Mexico City, where she was attending an engineering conference, and she had promised to cut short a visit to Istanbul, which she had planned to make immediately after a meeting in Athens.

Also, four of my brothers and their families, and my oldest sister Anne from California, and at least a couple of other sisters would be there too.

But before I was allowed to solo for two weeks with Teddy, both Mary and his nurse put me through a rather strenuous indoctrination, which included courses in dietetics, dress, sleeping habits, sanitation, laundry, medication, and beautification.

Frankly, I was concerned myself as to whether I could handle Teddy, and how he would fit into the Nantucket group. He was the youngest of the twenty-nine cousins, for one thing. And for another, my family is the only one from the South, and thus Teddy was perhaps more accustomed than the rest to being waited on by nurses.

At that time, Teddy had only recently graduated from Pablum, and he was still on other and miscellaneous canned and jarred foods for little children. Also he was—and still is—being dosed regularly with such tonics, vitamin extracts, and health supplements as cod-liver oil, fluoride, desiccated liver tablets, bone meal, yeast, and wheat germ.

Mary packed all of these—together with a pharmacopoeia of panaceas, elixirs, and medical devices running the gauntlet from thermometers to a hot-water bag with a full set of painful-looking appliances—in one rather ample valise.

Teddy had never been on an airplane before, or away from his mother and nurse. He kept assuring me that he wanted to fly. However, he always added one important qualification, which worried me somewhat. He'd point one chubby finger at the sky, and declaim, "But *certainly* not way up there, though."

I wondered what I'd do if he should freeze in terror after looking out the window of the plane. Or how I'd handle it if he should scream and kick or, even worse, become dreadfully airsick. And I was concerned, too, as to whether I'd have to take him to a rest room, en route.

When our departure date arrived, Mary and I had a change of heart, and we were tempted to call the whole thing off. I felt strong misgivings about being able to handle Teddy, and Mary felt equally strongly about entrusting her little darling to me. But we realized how disappointed he'd be, and besides my mother had rearranged her schedule for us. So we decided to go through with it.

The three of us drove to the Municipal Airport, with neither Mary nor I having much to say. I parked at the red curb in front of the waiting room, by a sign which said the space was positively reserved for official use only, and that the vehicles of violators would be towed away at their own expense.

One of the porters at the airport is a cousin of our yard-man, and he always looks out for us so I didn't worry about the sign. He is a gray-haired, balding, and handsome Negro named Herman Cohen. He came hurrying to help us from the car.

"Gracious peace, Teddy," he enthused as he started to remove suitcase after suitcase of gear from the car, "you going on a *real* trip, eh? I *know* you folks is going to enjoy Europe."

"We're only going up to Massachusetts, Herman," I told him. "And Mrs. Gilbreth isn't coming with us this time."

"All these bags for just you and Teddy?" he asked. "Go along!"

"Be extra careful of that bag, Herman," Mary warned, indicating the pharmacopoeia. "It's got some important bottles in it."

"Yes, ma'am," he chuckled. "I know that Mr. Gilbreth ain't going to travel hardly even across the street unless he have his important bottles."

Then, while we were waiting to board the plane, Mary gave me an oral refresher course on her long list of written instructions outlining how Teddy was to dress, what he was to eat, and what he was *not* to eat, when he was to be in bed, and how long he should stay in the sun and water. There were also some suggested menus, day by day, and some suggested outfits whose colors blended well so as to show him off to best advantage. Now that we were actually leaving, she was convinced again that she had made a terrible mistake to entrust a four-year-old to his father. And, for that matter, so was I.

She said goodbye to both of us as if she'd never see us again. Teddy *did* look mighty appealing in his Eton suit, with an Eton cap which had a tendency to rotate so that the bill was over an ear, like Jackie Coogan in *The Kid*.

I was dripping wet, from a combination of nervousness and the kind of weather that you get in Charleston in late August.

Teddy and I climbed up the ramp—and the fact that he required a good deal of urging, before he'd step into the plane, didn't make me feel any less nervous.

Once we got aboard, though, he didn't seem to be at all afraid. I had told him to watch for the man on the apron who held up fingers indicating that the pilot should start his engines. Teddy ran from one side of the plane to the other, bouncing over people's laps as he looked out the windows. Then holding up his own fingers, he issued terse orders to,

"Make this 'peller start going round." After that he blew idiot fashion through loose lips—a sort of limp-mouthed Bronx cheer—to imitate the sound of the motors.

When the plane started to taxi, I strapped him into his seat, and he waved to his mother. He was obviously gratified that the plane was doing its moving on the ground.

"*Certainly*, not way up there," he nodded hopefully to me, pointing in the general direction of the wild blue yonder.

Candidly, there are times, especially right at the beginning of a flight, when I rather agree with these sentiments myself. But I did my best to reassure him.

After we were airborne though, he didn't have the slightest sensation of being *certainly* way up there. And far from being airsick, he started to eat everything he could get his hands on. This was considerable, because the stewardess and even some of the female passengers kept stuffing him with ginger ale, cookies, colas, and sandwiches.

There wasn't any way I could stop them, without upsetting them badly and Ted even worse.

Now when a man is traveling by himself, most females wouldn't dream of changing their seats, so that they could move up next to him and start a conversation about personal matters. Well, perhaps I'd better say that when I'm traveling by myself it doesn't happen to me.

But there is something about traveling with a little boy that attracts women like flies. It seems to arouse the maternal instincts of even the most mannish, prudish, and reserved of females. They gather around interfering, simpering, posturing, grimacing, advising, and dangling goodies. They pump you about where you live, where you're going, and where you've been. If you take out a comb to fix the tyke's hair or a handkerchief to wipe his face, they want to do it for you. When he's asleep, they want to adjust the pillow under his head. When he's looking at pictures, they want to be sure he has enough light. And when he's eating, they want to cut his meat. You'd need a club to drive them away.

Our stewardess, a baby-faced brunette, also hovered around solicitously and Teddy took an immediate liking to her. After studying her for awhile he snapped his fingers—or at any rate tried to—and then announced triumphantly, "You're just like Shirley Temper."

The girl, who actually did look something like the former child movie star, flushed with pleasure. Teddy went on to explain to her that Miss "Temper" was one of his favorite television personalities, being out-ranked only by Lassie and Bugs Bunny. But the third-place rating didn't dim the girl's appreciation of the sincere compliment. And from then on, she redoubled her efforts to load down both him and me with snacks and assorted soft drinks.

It was a smooth and comfortably cool flight all the way to Idlewild Airport, and Teddy was much too interested in the plane and its passengers to become restless. After we had landed and taxied up to the terminal, he was reluctant to get off. But finally I talked him into it, by promising that we were taking another flight from New York to Nantucket.

On the apron at Idlewild, the sun was hot and blinding. Teddy hung back again, while he extracted the last mint from the last package—his fifth or sixth of the day. He was squint-eyed and tired, but flushed with excitement. It was the noisiest place and biggest crowd he had ever experienced, and he wasn't at all sure he trusted any part of it.

He put the mint in his mouth, let it get good and wet, took it out again, examined it, and then laid it flat on the top of his tongue. His hand was moistly sticky, so he reached over and wiped it on my trousers. It was still sticky when he hooked onto my forefinger.

"Holy mack'el," he said, "what a *place!*"

"Yeah," I agreed. "Come on, let's go inside where it's cool. We have to wait a couple of hours for the Nantucket plane."

"I don't feel like waiting."

"Neither do I," I agreed. "But there's not much we can do about it."

"I want some more candy."

"No more candy," I said automatically.

"I want to ride in an airplane. You *told* me we were going to ride in one."

"You just finished riding in one."

"I want to ride in *another* one."

"We're *going* to ride in another one. But first we have to wait until it's ready."

"But I want to ride right now."

"Not right now."

"Let's ride right now in this one over here," he insisted, picking a plane at random and trying to drag me to it.

"No, you can't get on just any plane. You have to find your own plane."

"Oh."

"So what do you want to do, walk around or sit down?"

"I want to get some candy."

"No more candy."

"Then I want to go to the bathroom."

"Are you sure?" I inquired tentatively.

"Yes."

"Okay, pal," I said with hearty assurance that I didn't feel. "I'm going to take you to a kind of bathroom you've never seen before. We'll find a men's room."

"What in the *world* is *that?*" he asked.

"It's where men go to the bathroom," I whispered.

"What about girls?" he demanded loudly. "Where do *they* go to the bathroom."

"Don't talk about it so loud," I begged, still whispering. "Girls go to a place called the ladies' room."

"I don't want to go to any old men's room," he decided.

"Well, you certainly can't go to the ladies' room," I told him desperately.

"Then I think I'll go right here—right now."

"Not right here or right now," I implored in horrified

tones. "Give me a break, kid! Give me a break! Wait a few minutes. You'll *like* the men's room. I promise you that you will. Man, you'll *love* it."

"Where is it, then?" he asked impatiently.

"Well, first we have to *find* it," I conceded.

"And we have to find some candy, too, don't we, Daddy?"

I have never been slow to recognize a blackmail pitch, but I was more than willing to capitulate. "Right, boy," I told him. "You're right as rain."

A boy's first visit to the men's room—like his first visit to an all-male barbershop—is an important milestone on the road to manhood.

I vividly remember my father taking me. Although he understood every detail of the most complicated pieces of machinery, he always had trouble doping out the intricacies of a small boy's clothes. And while he hunted frantically for buttons, hooks-and-eyes, cleverly concealed apertures, and secret little flaps, I danced impatiently from foot to foot.

The men's room at Idlewild was packed, and Teddy cased the room quickly, in wide-eyed distrust. "Greaat Gawd," he remarked in his thickest Charleston brogue, "what in the world kind of a place is *this?*"

"It's an all-right place," I assured him. "This is the place I was telling you about—a men's room."

"Gracious Gawd," he varied the oath only slightly. "Why do they all want to go at the same time, eh Daddy?"

I didn't know what answer to give to that one—or to some

of the subsequent ones.

"This room is no *good* for you," he finally told me, arriving again at the verdict usually reserved for parsnips, afternoon naps, shampoos, and polio shots.

"Sure it is," I chuckled with false heartiness. "It's a first-rate room . . ."

Everything went reasonably smoothly, after all. But you could tell that Teddy didn't trust the place, and that he was actually afraid.

The thing he liked least of all was a machine to dry your hands—the kind where you push a knob, and the machine gives a tired sigh and exhales tepid air, while you rub your hands briskly.

Teddy took a few steps toward the drier. But every time a patron pushed the knob and caused it to exhale, my son cringed away from it and held his ears to block out the frighteningly human sound.

"She won't scare," he told me. It was a plain statement of fact but he didn't believe a word of it.

"Heck no, Teddy Boy," I said, stepping up to the machine, while he pulled at my pants. "Look here. All I do is press this knob and . . . Whoosh! Out comes the warm air. There is something inside like an electric fan, I guess. See? Look, I'll press it again. Whoosh! Isn't that fun?"

"Whoosh," he replied gravely. Just the same, he didn't think it was fun, and he still held his ears.

I washed the sticky mint juice off his hands, and tried to

clean him up the best I could. Since he refused to put his hands under the drier, I used a handkerchief as a towel.

"It's no *good* for you," he repeated, keeping a safe distance from the machine.

I wondered what my father would have done, faced with the same situation. Probably he would have grabbed me and held my hands under the drier, while I howled, to show me there was no reason to be frightened.

But I never have believed in combating fright with terror— in heaving the child off the springboard just because he's afraid to get his big toe wet.

I was debating what I ought to try next with Ted, when the dilemma was postponed by a rather youthful, large, and rough-looking man behind me.

"Hey, Mac," he glowered, gesturing with wet hands, "that machine ain't no toy, you know. You pushed it twict, already. Now give somebody else a chanct, for Crissake. Move!"

There was a time, twenty or thirty years ago, when I would have felt duty-bound to make this rough-looking individual a sincere little speech. No one likes to be bullied in front of his son. So perhaps I would have matched rudeness with rudeness, and suggested that my tormentor go twist himself head-deep into a block of wood. Or I might have implied that he was too abysmally stupid to distinguish between his elbow and other parts of his anatomy.

That sort of speech can very well be delivered by a young

man who is prepared to defend his honor; or by an old man who knows he won't have to.

But not by a middle-aged man—or at any rate not by *this* one.

If middle-aged men want to stay out of trouble, they must develop a philosophy which will allow them to swallow insults. For the plain truth is that they are neither young enough nor old enough to be immune from abuse. My own particular ploy nowadays is to confuse the opposition with such exaggerated politeness that it doesn't know whether to apologize or take a poke at me.

"Oh, excuse me, sir," I gushed in my most honeyed voice. "I'm terribly sorry. I didn't realize I was delaying anyone. What a nuisance I must seem! Here, step right up, sir. And please allow me!"

I pressed the knob of the machine for him, but instead of stepping up, he backed hastily away.

"Never mind, Mac," he grumbled, as he headed for the door. "My hands are dry already."

I turned to Teddy, and he was holding his ears again, to drown out the "whoosh."

"Let's go," I told him. "Never mind the machine. If it scares you, you'll outgrow it someday."

"She won't scare me," he said, taking my hand. "Why did that man call you 'Mac,' Daddy?"

"Oh, I don't know. Just sort of a nickname, I guess."

"Did he talk mean to you?"

"Maybe so. But you saw me get rid of him, didn't you?"

"Did he want to use the whoosh-machine?"

"Yes, but I wouldn't let him. You saw me fix his wagon."

"Good boy, Daddy!"

I thought somewhat sourly that if Teddy were timid, he surely came by it naturally.

"Come on," I told him almost roughly, "let's get out of here."

"Okay, Mac," he grinned.

"Mr. Mac to you, small fry," I corrected him.

CHAPTER 5

NEW NURSE

IT IS TRADITION IN MY FAMILY TO MUSTER ALL HANDS FOR A big greeting, when any one of us arrives on Nantucket. If you are coming by steamer from Woods Hole, the clan will line Brant Point to wave you in. If you are flying, the clan converges on the little airport near South Shore, where we used to pick blueberries as children.

Whoever chose the site of the airport picked the worst spot on the whole island, from a weather standpoint. The

landing field is on the former Nobadeer Farm property, and
the fog invariably comes there first, and leaves last. The re-
sult is that more flights are canceled than not—or at least
that's the way it seems when you run into a foggy spell.

The weather was clear and beautiful, though, on the afternoon Teddy and I flew in. We were met by three automobiles
containing seventeen people; Sancho Panza and Bonnie,
dogs; James, a cat; and Charlie, a caged parakeet, which has
never talked, perhaps because he never had a fair chance.
There were more animals where those came from, but that
was the extent of the furred and feathered friends which
either had leaped or were carried into the vehicles, as the clan
—usually five or ten minutes behind schedule—departed
with haste from the cottages.

These enthusiastic and noisy welcomes tend to overwhelm
even a veteran family-reunioner like me. So it's understand-
able that Teddy was somewhat bewildered.

The only one of the group he had ever seen before was
my mother, who had visited us a number of times in Charleston, usually en route to or from various speaking engage-
ments.

Still, Teddy was nothing like as shy as I was afraid he
might be. During the flight from New York, I had coached
him on the desirability of shaking hands warmly all around
—with a firm grip and looking the other person squarely in
the eye.

He went through the motions of shaking hands, all right.

And if he didn't quite manage to look everyone in the eye, at least he didn't turn his head too far away over his shoulder, or try to hide behind me.

Mother and the girls—all old pros when it comes to handling children—had sense enough not to yield to the all-but-irresistible temptation of covering him with kisses.

"Gracious Gawd," drawled Teddy, after he had finally made the rounds, "do we have to shake hands all day? I never shook hands with so many head of people in all my bored days."

"Gracious Gawd," tittered one of his teen-age cousins from New Jersey. "Listen to that Rebel!"

"Don't tease him," the cousin's mother warned.

"Why do all the aunts and uncles on Nantucket want to talk so funny?" Teddy asked me.

"Maybe they think *you* talk funny?" I told him.

"*Whaaat?*" he asked incredulously. The modulation for this word, incidentally, comes directly from our yard-man. He starts the word with normal pitch, and then rides up the scale like a siren to a high-C whinny. It's part of a special act that he puts on for Teddy, and he uses it whenever my son announces an important scoop like the sighting of a butterfly.

Even Mother laughed at Teddy now, although she quickly assured the child that they weren't making fun of him.

We waited around some more, while a couple of my brothers claimed my luggage for me, and of course there were some remarks about its volume. Then we wandered over to the car. Teddy squealed with glee when he saw the assorted pets confined therein.

"A dog, another dog, a bird *and*," he chortled in ecstasy, "a cat."

"Do you have a cat, Teddy?" one of my sisters asked.

"Not quite," he replied. "But my Daddy's going to get me one as a ward."

"As a *ward?*" she repeated. "What do you mean by that, Teddy?"

"A ward, that's all," he said.

"What does he mean by a 'ward'?" she asked me.

I knew all right, but since I hadn't broken the news about the forthcoming Little Stranger, I tried to change the subject. "Search me," I said. "Come on, let's go."

"A ward?" she persisted. "Oh, I think I've got it. Teddy, do you mean a *re*-ward?"

"Yes."

"So your Daddy's going to get you a cat for a reward," she said, pleased with her acumen. "A reward for *what?*"

"Let's get going, eh?" I put in. "Come on, Ted, climb into one of the cars."

But by now, everyone was interested in finding out what sort of an achievement on Ted's part would merit the gift of a cat. So no one paid any attention to me.

"As a ward for letting Mama have a new baby," he announced.

"Ah-ha!" my sister gloated, proud of having pumped out the news.

"Whaaat?" imitated one of my brothers. And I found myself blushing in spite of myself. Everybody likes to tease a middle-aged father.

"Okay, wise guy," was the best I could mutter.

"Why I think that's wonderful!" my mother said enthusiastically. Everyone knew that, freely translated, her remark meant, "All right, now, enough's enough. Lay off of him." So there was no further levity at the expense of the Charleston contingent.

Naturally, I also thought it was wonderful news. But I could have wrung Teddy's neck—and everyone else's too, for that matter.

I rode with my mother in Jack's car, and Teddy surprised me by deciding to go with Dan. The reason for this decision, it turned out, was James, the cat. My son lay in the back of Dan's station-wagon, and cuddled the old cat in his arms. If James objected, he was too old or lazy to extricate himself, and too gentle to protest.

It had been a long trip from Charleston, and the boy was asleep by the time we reached my mother's cottage, The Shoe, where he and I had been given my usual room.

Dan carried Teddy in for me, and I dumped him onto one of the twin beds, so that he could finish his nap before supper. At home, he always slept in a crib, and I hoped he wouldn't roll out. The Eton suit, which had been spotless that morning, now looked as if he had been leaning against too many sticky wickets, or something.

My mother came tiptoeing in to help me unpack, and the first bag she opened was the valise containing all the medicines. For a moment, it gave her a start, and then she was all sympathy—or pretended to be.

"Why you poor dear," she whispered, "is it serious? Why didn't you write me about it?"

It is always hard for me to tell whether she's needling me —and I still don't know for sure, in this particular case. I suspect that she was. But on the other hand, if she wasn't, I certainly didn't want to be impolite.

"There's nothing the matter with me," I replied, deciding to play it cautiously down the middle. "All that stuff is for Teddy."

"For *Teddy*," she gasped. "Oh, what a shame! I'll make him some milk toast. And we'd certainly better keep him away from the other children."

"Well, there's nothing really the *matter* with him," I admitted.

"There isn't? Then . . ."

"That's just his vitamins, and all."

"Oh," she commented, picking up a portable croup kettle, and examining it.

"And," I explained, "things to use in case something should *get* to be the matter with him."

"I see," she nodded so noncommittally that my suspicions were definitely aroused again.

"Say, are you taking me for a ride?" I inquired, perhaps snapping a little, because I was tired, too. And, besides, snapping at parents is a privilege which children never entirely outgrow, regardless of how old they become.

"What do you mean?" she asked so innocently that I decided I might be doing her an injustice. "A ride about what?"

"Never mind," I dismissed the idea. "I'm sorry. It's been a long day."

"Perhaps I'd better fix some milk toast for *you.*"

I recognized that as a mild reprimand for my bad manners, which by implication she was now attributing to indisposition. Mother knows next-to-nothing about cooking, but she has always been very proud of the few dishes she *does* know how to prepare. It is certainly not my intention here to injure her feelings, so all I will say is that I have had her milk toast on numerous occasions in the past, and if a person isn't sick before he eats it, he may very well be afterwards. Also, having seldom been sick herself in more than fourscore years, she seems to believe that a couple of servings of milk toast should be sufficient to put almost any patient on the road to recovery; and that any lurking around in bed after such feasting—to allow a broken neck to heal or scarlet fever to go away—may well amount to malingering.

"I tell you what I'll do, Mother," I said. "You fix a big

batch of milk toast, and I'll *divide* it with you."

"Not for me, thanks, although you tempt me, dear," she said placidly.

Teddy woke up in a good humor, about an hour-and-a-half later and in plenty of time for supper. He and I had a shower together, down in the boy's bathroom. That was his first shower, and he liked it so well that he wanted to hog all the water, while I stood in the boondocks at the back of the stall and shivered.

We walked back to our room swathed in Turkish towels. I laid out some clothes for him, and he did a pretty good job of dressing himself, although he got his polo shirt and his training pants on backwards.

He obviously didn't like the idea of having to make decision after decision—racking his brain—about which foot went where and which arm went through which hole. And a few minutes later, when my mother and some of the girls were admiring him, he decided to do something about it.

"Well," he drawled, "who's going to be my nurse?"

When they smiled and stood mute, instead of hastening to volunteer for the honor, he repeated pleasantly enough, but a bit pompously:

"I *said*, who's going to be my nurse?"

"You don't have a nurse here," I explained.

"Go along!"

"In Nantucket," I added, "*nobody* has a nurse."

"Whaaat?"

"That's right."

"Then," he choked, and his eyes filled with tears, "if Mama's not here, who's going to look out for me?"

"When you need help," I assured him, "I'll be your nurse."

"Gracious Gawd," he sniffed indignantly, "you don't know a blessed *thing* about that."

"Sure I do," I insisted. "Didn't I bring you all the way from Charleston?"

"But a boy needs a *lady* nurse. Everybody knows that, by granny!"

My mother and the girls quickly promised that they'd all be his nurses, whenever he wanted one. He thought that over for a moment, and decided to put them to the test.

"All right, then," he said, pointing to his feet, "who wants to tie my shoes?"

"I do," Mother volunteered. Still spry as a young woman, she kneeled beside him on the straw rug. "Oh, goodness, Teddy, you've got them on the wrong feet!"

"I *always* do that," he conceded.

"Well let's fix them."

"All right," he said, and you could tell he was beginning to conclude that his grandmother knew her business after all, and might yet make a satisfactory flunky.

He lifted one foot, so that she could slip off the shoe, and he steadied himself by putting both hands on top of her head.

I remember when my mother had thick, dark, red hair,

which hung below her waist. In Providence, a hairdresser used to come to the house once a week, and shampoo it. Mother wore her hair all wound up in a pile, on the top of her head. But right after supper every night, she'd take it down and brush it.

While she read aloud to us children for an hour or so, Anne, Ernestine, and Martha would take turns massaging some sort of spicy-smelling tonic into her scalp. Then the girls would plait her hair into two long, heavy braids. And by the time that job was finished, it would be my bedtime.

Mother's hair now is white, and of course it is not as thick as it used to be back in the days when she was a pretty thing with seven young children, and studying for her Ph. D. But Teddy patted her head much as my older sisters used to, when they were rubbing in tonic. Then, he said for the second time that day,

"Just like Shirley Temper."

"Why you flatterer!" Mother chided him, "You Southern men are all alike, Teddy."

CHAPTER 6

HIGH OLD TIME

THE ADULT MEMBERS OF THE FAMILY GATHERED AT THE
Shoe that evening for cocktails; and the children, including
Teddy, were temporarily banished from the premises. He
was wide awake, after his nap and shower, and he had eaten
so much candy on the flight that I figured he wouldn't be
hungry until I was ready to feed him. They took him over
to Dan's house, where the children were having some sort of
a gala.

Although my mother attended the cocktail party, she neither gave it nor indulged in it. She doesn't drink and, to the best of my knowledge, has never tasted the stuff, or taken a puff from a nasty old coffin-nail, either.

I don't say that she is prudish about drinking. It is simply that she is convinced, even at this time of life, that while *some* people may be able to handle booze in moderation, one sip would make a slave of her.

And I think she believes implicitly that it would only be a matter of time, after that, when she'd be on the downward path: First a convivial cocktail or two before dinner, next martinis at lunch, and a pick-me-up in the morning. Next secret tippling, a half-pint in the pocketbook, and switching to vodka so that no one would smell the stuff on her breath. Then, all-day drinking bouts. Arrested and thrown into the Black Maria for being drunk and disorderly. And, finally, broke and friendless, drinking Sterno with the other pitiful derelicts on Skid Row.

I certainly am not going to imply, though, that she's a wet blanket at a family cocktail party. That might be considered disrespectful—and, even at my age, I am not deemed too old to be skinned alive.

Of course, it is just a matter of factual reporting to record that she *does* start wondering aloud whether it isn't time to eat, coincident with the removal of the first tray of ice cubes.

Then, with bustling efficiency, she busies herself emptying ashtrays, confiscating olives, removing glasses, and re-corking bottles. Meanwhile, she's turned the oven and all the burners on the stove to full blast, so she can allege that the dalliance over drinks is causing the dinner to burn.

Right from the beginning of a cocktail party, any empty glass is considered fair game for her removal. And after the party is ten minutes old, any untended glass, empty or not, becomes fair game. If you're unlucky enough to get a late start—and thoughtlessly put your first drink down after just one sip—the place to look for your glass is in the dishwasher.

Also, she has a habit of grasping the elbow of any toper who has taken a second drink. I'm not exactly sure what the purpose is, but I think the general idea is to support the dissipated wretch, so that he won't fall down in a heap, right in the middle of her living room. Anyway, it is mighty disconcerting.

Whenever I'm staying at her house and manage to keep my glass long enough to have that second cocktail, she's fairly certain to ask me the next morning if I don't want to remain in bed for awhile. She doesn't add, "and sleep it off" —but that's the implication. Sometimes, too, she'll bring black coffee to my bedroom, for the headache she assumes is plaguing me. It does no good to protest that I don't have a headache, because she gives me a look that says she'll have to hand me one thing, anyway: I still know how to keep a stiff upper lip, and suffer in silence.

I'm sure that if anyone had *three* cocktails before supper, milk toast would appear in the morning along with the black coffee. A sobering thought!

When we have cocktail parties at The Shoe, we ourselves provide the ingredients. Mother has never given a cocktail party for anyone, least of all her own children.

Right after my brothers and I were released from the service after World War II, she *did* break down and give a beer party. Twenty people came, and there were twelve bottles of beer in the icebox—more than enough, as she pointed out, for everyone to have almost a full glass.

I'm never entirely sure just how much Twentieth Century slang my mother really understands, because she hardly ever uses it herself. But she has an astronomer friend of long standing at Nantucket, who invariably asks her whether we "children" are having a "high old time" on vacation. And, just as invariably, Mother purses her lips and replies that, yes *indeed,* we certainly are.

That night at The Shoe, we had time for only one drink, because by then everything was boiling over on the stove, and you could smell the swordfish starting to char on the oven grill. While my mother secreted the highball glasses in the dishwasher, I went into the yard and called over to Dan's house, for Teddy to come to supper.

He came promptly enough, and I had some cornflakes, applesauce, and milk on the table for him.

Supper is ordinarily not his best meal. He eats a fairly good breakfast and quite a big lunch, but he dawdles over supper—even though it's always pretty light fare.

He drank most of his milk, and ate some of his applesauce, but I couldn't get him to touch the cornflakes. I knew that Mary would be upset, if she telephoned and found that he wasn't eating. So I employed every trick that I had ever seen Mary or his nurse use, in a desperate attempt to get the cereal down him.

"Open your mouth and close your eyes," I said, "and I'll give you something . . ."

"No, thanks," Teddy interrupted me firmly, "I'm not hungry."

"I tell you what," I said. "Eat just three teaspoons full."

"No."

"Eat two, then."

"No."

"As a personal favor to me!"

"No."

Usually, if Mary could get him to agree to eat as many as two teaspoons full, she could get almost the whole bowl down him, by giving him a long and crooked count, "One, one and an eighth, one and a seventh, one and a sixth," and so forth, topped off finally with a triumphant, "Twoooo!" But that night, Teddy held firm against any cereal whatsoever.

"If he's not hungry, he's not hungry," one of my sisters pointed out. "They probably had something to eat over at Dan's, anyway."

"He's *got* to eat his cereal," I insisted. "Please, Teddy!"

"No," he said.

"See if he'll eat for you," I asked my mother.

"If he doesn't want to eat, I wouldn't make him," she said.

"What about some go-ghees?" Teddy asked.

"Good idea," I enthused, wondering why I hadn't thought about them myself. "If I put some go-ghees on the cereal, will you eat it?"

"I think so," he promised.

"Good deal. I'll see if there are any in the kitchen."

Mother and the others at the table had been following the conversation with interest.

"I can tell you right now," one of my brothers reported, "there is not a single go-ghee in the house."

"There isn't?" I asked, and I was mighty disappointed. "Do you think any of the stores are still open?"

"Don't tell me," he said, "that you plan to ride all the way into town just to get a . . . By the way, just what *are* go-ghees?"

"They're what Teddy calls raisins," I explained impatiently.

"That makes sense," he remarked. "Does he have any other special vocabulary that we ought to know?"

"Well, let's see," I said absently, still holding a teaspoon of cornflakes in front of Teddy's tightly clamped mouth, "you'd have to ask Mary for the whole list. Carrots are 'toddues' and ice cream is 'rimmer.' Then . . ."

"Say, isn't that *precious!*" he interrupted.

I put down the teaspoon and looked irately around the table. Everyone was smirking, and I wasn't in the mood for it.

"And," Teddy continued, "Mama and I call mashed potatoes 'mashies.' And pajamas are 'jommies,' eh Daddy?"

"Skip it," I ordered. "I don't want to hear another word out of you until you eat your supper. Incidentally," I asked my mother, "do we have any raisins in the house?"

"I'm sorry, but we don't," she said. "I'll be sure to get some tomorrow, though."

"What's a hot dog, Granddear?" Teddy asked my mother, using the name that all her grandchildren call her.

"It's a sausage," she explained.

"I had *three* hot dogs over at Uncle Dan's," he confided. "We cooked them outside, with some marshmows and gingerale."

"Three hot dogs," I yelped. "Ye gads, boy! You've never had a hot dog in your life!"

"He has *now*," the same brother who had quizzed about the go-ghees pointed out. "And what's a 'marshmow' in Teddy-Mary language?"

"You got me," I conceded. "What's a marshmow, Teddy?"

"A little white ball that you put over the fire on a stick."

"Marshmallow," Mother nodded. "I remember how you all used to like them, when you were children."

"Three hot dogs," I moaned. "If Mary telephones, not a

word from anyone!"

"I don't believe they'll hurt him," my mother predicted. "He must have been hungry after that long trip, poor dear."

About that time, a Bermuda bell sounded loud and clear from the sand road outside. And at this Pied-Piper call, assorted cousins—in various forms of nightdress—converged on an ice-cream wagon which parked out front in the gathering dusk.

"Gracious peace, what's that?" Teddy inquired.

"The 'toddues' man," said my brother.

"Who wants toddues!" Teddy asked scornfully. "Not me, eh Dad? I'm too full."

"Your uncle is all mixed up," I told the boy. "That's not 'toddues.' That's 'rimmer.' "

"Oh, *do!*" said Teddy, which is Charlestonese for "stop joking."

"I mean it. You give the man a dime, and he gives you 'rimmer.' "

"Whaaat?" Obviously that was his idea of real luxury. "You mean they *bring* it to you?"

"Right."

"I want some."

"After all those hot dogs? And marshmallows?"

"Yes."

Everyone was looking at me, to see what I'd do. It certainly didn't seem fair for all of the children to have dessert but him. I mulled over the matter for a few moments, and then fished in my pocket for a dime.

While he was eating the ice cream, I checked to see whether Mary had given me any written instructions about stomachaches or whether, by any chance, she had remembered to pack a stomach pump.

She hadn't, but in any event, neither the instructions nor the pump was needed. Teddy went right to bed, and slept soundly. By the time I got up the next morning, a couple of older cousins had already taken him for a pre-breakfast swim. Then he had a date for pancakes, over at his Cousin Davie's house.

CHAPTER 7

POISON IVY

I DIDN'T SEE TEDDY AGAIN UNTIL LUNCHTIME, WHEN HE came home sunburned and hungry. The burn wasn't severe, though, because someone had kept him coated with oil. There's a reciprocal agreement that whenever you see a pink child playing in a group of brown ones, you pull him out of circulation long enough to anoint him, and send him home if the pink threatens to turn red.

So I wasn't worried about sunstroke, drowning, or anything else serious, since I knew that adequate family rules and precautions had been in effect since I was a boy.

However, I *was* worried about poison ivy, which thrives around The Shoe.

It would have been borrowing trouble, as they say in New England, to have mentioned the poison ivy problem to Mary. And she had been so busy issuing advisories about the prevention of major tragedies—like where to apply the tourniquet—that she hadn't thought of it herself.

But it was very much on my mind. I've seen holidays utterly ruined on account of the malady. It has been my experience that one scratching, whining, fretful child can sabotage the vacations of everyone in the house.

In view of the fact that I return to Nantucket every summer, it should be unnecessary for me to say that I think it's a delightful island. Still, it *is* true that soil and climatic conditions there seem to be ideal for poison ivy. The bush rises to majestic heights in sandy fields where little else except hardy wild roses will grow. As early as mid-July its handsome, glossy leaves begin to turn crimson. By August, the whole plant is magnificently aflame. I suppose Nantucket is one of the few places in the world where vacationers actually gather in droves to admire the poison ivy.

From time to time, the island fathers have authorized the spending of tax funds for chemical sprays and other eradication programs. But so far no St. Patrick has emerged who is able to rid Nantucket of the itch. To date, the various programs have succeeded only in splitting the summer colony down the middle.

For instance, the bird-lovers warn that elimination of the bush might not sit at all well with our feathered friends, possibly causing them all to migrate. And without birds, there'd be a mosquito epidemic.

The hay-fever sufferers say they wish to God the authorities would stop throwing away money on such boondoggles as itch-eradication, and concentrate on getting rid of the ragweed.

And the low-tax advocates ask rhetorically whether, if the good Lord in His infinite wisdom had wanted Nantucket to be free of poison ivy, he would not have seen to it that the island was *created* free of it.

Be that as it may, I proceeded to give Teddy a full indoctrination course on both the recognition and avoidance of the noxious weed. After lunch that day, I took him outside and showed him the bushes from a safe distance.

"If you even get *close* to one of those bushes with the red leaves," I told him sternly, "it's going to be like a thousand mosquito bites. You'll feel terrible, you won't be able to go swimming, and the doctor may have to come and give you a shot."

"I don't want no shots," he said in some alarm, edging away from me in distrust. "Absolutely not!"

"I don't want you to have one, either," I assured him. "You know I *hate* to make you have shots."

I don't think he quite believed that, though. Sometimes he appears convinced that the real purpose of his shots is to titillate my sadistic instincts, since I'm the one who used to have the privilege of holding him down while the doctor injected the needle. And in this specific case, I'm afraid he thought the poison ivy was just a figment of my cruel imagination—something I was going to use as an excuse to call the doctor, so that I could get my kicks.

"Shots aren't no *good* for you," he told me, edging away still further, and preparing to make a break for it, if I should attempt to grab him.

I'm sure it's bad psychology to use the threat of shots as a deterrent. But I made an exception this time. I surely didn't want him to be miserable for his whole vacation, so drastic measures seemed warranted.

"You keep away from those bushes with the red leaves," I warned, "or the doctor will come here with his great big needle. And you know what happens then! Jab!" I jabbed with an imaginary syringe, and he winced.

"I'll bet they don't have no needles on Nantucket," he said, trying to feel me out. "*Do* don't say that!"

"The heck they don't," I told him. "Man, don't you know that they have some of the biggest needles in the country, right here on the island?"

"Oh," he said thoughtfully, and I knew I had him worried. "How big?"

I held the palms of my hands about eighteen inches apart.

"Holy mack'el," he gulped.

"You said it!" I agreed. "Now just be careful, that's all."

I asked the other children to help me keep him out of the bushes, and they promised to do their best. But I wasn't at

all sure that the precautions would work. I knew he was convinced for the time being of the danger involved, and I knew
also that he wouldn't openly defy me. But there wasn't any
guarantee that he'd remember what I told him, or that he
wouldn't brush up against the weed by mistake.

As it turned out, my fears were amply justified. Late that
afternoon, when I returned from a sail with three of my
brothers, we were horrified to find Teddy standing half-
naked, right in the middle of a prize-taking poison-ivy bush
not quite as large as a California redwood.

By half-naked, I mean that he was wearing only his drum
bathing suit. This was a garment Mary had seen a couple
of years before in New York, and had thought it so cute that
she bought it on the spot, even knowing that he'd have to
grow into it. The sides of the bathing suit were made to look
like a drum, and they covered about four inches of Teddy's
middle. Since four-year-old boys don't have hips, the trunks
were held aloft by a single strap. He had on no shoes, socks,
or shirt.

"Teddy," I screamed in a mixture of fright and rage,
"what are you *doing,* you naughty boy!"

He held up a beach pail almost full of the red seed pods
of wild roses.

"Look, Daddy," he said unabashed, "I'm picking tomatoes
for Granddear."

"Get out of there!" I hollered. "Quick!"

"Can't you see I'm busy right now," he pointed out patiently. "We're going to have a great big tomato salad for supper."

"You're going to have a great big needle stuck in you," I groaned. "Oh, Lord, why did I ever bring you with me in the first place."

The threat of the needle brought him out of the bushes. There was one sprig of poison ivy sticking in the waistband of the bathing trunks, and a couple of leaves were glued moistly to his back. There were also quite a few stray leaves in with the "tomatoes."

I dusted him off as best I could, dragged him into The Shoe, and called the island's pediatrician—an overworked chap who, I guess, has had as much experience as any man alive in removing splinters, treating sunstroke, draining ears, taking the sand out of clam-shell cuts, and prescribing for poison ivy.

The doctor wasn't very hopeful, but he recommended an immediate bath with plenty of soap. And he said that when the rash appeared, I should bring Teddy down for a shot that would minimize the itching.

Although I figured that the harm was done, I couldn't resist lecturing Teddy on the wages of sin.

"Now when you start to itch, young man, don't blame me," I told him. "Remember, I warned you over and over again to stay out of the stuff."

"If I itch, I'll scratch, that's all," he promised.

"But did you pay any attention to my warnings?" I droned on. "Not the slightest! The first time I turned my back, where did I find you? Up to your ears in the biggest bush on the whole island. Well, it won't be any use for you to gripe to *me* about itching. If there's anything I can't stand, it's a griper."

"Me, too," Teddy agreed, a little too enthusiastically.

"I'm not griping," I corrected him firmly. "I'm merely pointing out that when you don't do what I tell you, you can expect to pay the consequences. That's all."

"I hate gripers, don't you, Daddy?"

"I surely do," I agreed. "I despise them."

Meanwhile, every few hours, I'd pull up his shirt and examine him for a rash. I thought the most likely place to find it would be on his stomach, where the sprig had caught in his waistband.

Finally, during one examination, Teddy himself discovered the telltale rash. But instead of being on him, it was on the back of my right hand.

I'd never had poison ivy before in my life. I've been head high in it, inadvertently, chasing tennis and golf balls, and never caught it. I've cut the stuff with a rotary mower and dug it up with a spade, and never caught it. But that summer I caught poison ivy, and made up for lost time. I suppose the contact came when I was brushing the leaves off Teddy.

Either he's immune, or the immediate bath and soap did the trick, because he came through unscathed. And although he was half-naked and I was fully clothed I got it all over my body.

"Just don't gripe about it, please!" he had the nerve to tell me, on the infrequent occasions when my Spartan reserve broke down enough for me to gasp that the itch was driving me crazy, and that by comparison Job's boils were no more than acne.

Although Mary had not specifically mentioned the danger of poison ivy, she had shown the foresight to include a large economy vat of calamine lotion, in Teddy's medicine kit. When it became clear that he wouldn't need it, I appropriated it to my own uses. Even so, for six or seven days I was in misery, and hardly slept a wink.

Far from sympathizing, Teddy alleged that my scratching and rolling around in bed kept him awake all night.

"Daddy, you make me a nervous wreck!" he reproved me.

He also had the gall to insist that, for my own good, I ought to call the doctor and have an injection.

"Believe me, boy," I told him righteously, "if it would do me any good at all, I'd have the needle in a hurry. Anything would be better than this constant itching."

"After this," he said, "you'll keep away from poison ivy, eh Daddy? She's no *good* for you."

"Yes, sir," I continued, "all the doctor has to do is say the word about the needle and I'll be ready."

"Can I hold you down?"

"I don't need anybody to hold me down," I said with some dignity.

"Well, can I watch, then? Can I, Daddy?"

"No, blast it all," I shouted, with my feelings hurt in spite of myself, "you can't! What do you think it is, a free show or something?"

"I don't never have no fun," he whined, almost in tears.

"Blast it all," I repeated, "here I get poison ivy trying to take care of you, and all you want to do is watch your poor old daddy suffer!"

"Well, I didn't get no poison ivy," he pointed out. "I was a *good* boy, wasn't I, Daddy?"

"I guess so," I capitulated, tired of the argument.

"So can I watch you get a shot, then?"

"You can watch me cut my throat from ear to ear, if you don't shut up," I whinnied, now utterly exasperated.

My mother arrived at that point, with a tray of milk toast.

"What are you shouting at Teddy about?" she reproved me.

"Nothing," I sighed. "And I don't like to be irritable, but you can take that graveyard stew right back to the kitchen."

"What my Daddy needs," Teddy volunteered, "is to drive downtown and have a shot—a great big shot."

"Boy," I agreed enthusiastically for Mother's benefit, "you can say *that* again."

"No, Teddy," said my Mother. "I don't like to disagree

with you, but that is exactly what he does *not* need."

"Gripe, gripe, gripe all day, eh Granddear?" he asked in the long-suffering tones of a saint who is being tried.

"Exactly," she agreed.

CHAPTER 8

LOOSE TOOTH

AFTER A FEW MORE DAYS AT NANTUCKET, TEDDY FITTED SO naturally into the tribe that no one but me paid any especial attention to him. Originally, that's exactly what I had hoped would happen, for his own good, since he had to get accustomed to sharing the spotlight. Still, when it actually *did* happen, I couldn't help but resent it. Surely my brothers, sisters, and mother weren't so unobservant as to think that my son was just another member of the group!

Even after I discovered that he had developed his first loose tooth, the news didn't burst like a bombshell when I mentioned it at dinner. As I recall, one sister said that *her* youngest boy didn't lose a tooth until he was five; one brother asked me if I had noticed his seven-year-old daughter—that she was at the stage where she hardly had a tooth in her head; and another brother said that reminded him: he had to go to the dentist when he got back to Montclair, and that while he hadn't any cavities the *last* time, the time before he had . . .

Anyway, only my mother remembered to look at Teddy's tooth. And, while I don't intend to be critical, I thought that even her examination bordered on the cursory.

The loose tooth was a big deal to Teddy, though. He wouldn't allow me to touch it, let alone help him to pull it out, and he went around with his finger in his mouth, gently rocking the tooth back and forth.

Of course it's true, as the cynics persist in pointing out, that the chemistry of death begins at birth. And if you want to consider things in that gloomy light, losing the first tooth is *another* all-important milestone in the life of a child. But, believe me, no one at The Shoe wanted to take the trouble of considering it in that light—or any other light, either.

The same casualness toward loose teeth prevailed in the family, when I was a boy. Almost every day, some child was either teething or losing same. And my father used to complain to Mother that the Good Fairy, who left a nickel under your pillow in return for a tooth wrapped in tissue paper, was going to put him in debtors' prison.

So even I didn't think Teddy's tooth was much of an attention-getter. But I *did* happen to mention it casually in a postcard to Mary, which was devoted for the most part to a graphic description of my poison ivy, and how it was killing me.

It took two days for the postcard to reach the Holy City, and be delivered to our house. And about thirty seconds later, Mary had completed a telephone call to The Shoe.

"Well, which tooth *is* it, anyway?" she asked almost breathlessly. "I can't get over it!"

"Four years old, and starting to wear out already," I teased her.

"Imagine it! About to lose a tooth!"

"It surely is good to hear your voice," I said, falling back on the sort of platitudes reserved for unexpected long-distance calls, especially when the house is full of people. "Say, how's the weather down there? You wouldn't believe it, but we slept under two blankets last night. And I mean *heavy* blankets. By the way, the rates are lower after six o'clock, you know."

"You didn't expect me to wait until *then,* did you? Is he feeling all right? Which tooth? Don't you think you'd better take him to a dentist, just to be sure everything's going all right?"

"I don't believe he needs a dentist," I said. "It would just be throwing away money. I'm sure everything's fine."

"Well, *which* tooth?"

"Oh, I don't know. One of his lowers, I think. Gad, you ought to see my poison ivy. Honestly, from head to toe . . ."

"A *lower*," she exclaimed as if there were a good deal more than two possibilities. "Well, isn't that wonderful! Does he like it in Nantucket? *Which* lower?"

"He's right here. It's a lower, all right. Sort of a little right of center. I've got a lotion on this stuff, and I think I'll be able to go swimming again . . ."

"On *what* stuff?" she asked suspiciously. "What's happened to him?"

"It's not him. I'm still talking about my poison ivy."

"Oh. Yes, that's a terrible shame. You're being careful to keep *him* out of it, aren't you? Which lower did you say?"

"It's the one just right of center."

"Oh, *that* lower. Are you sure?"

"Well, he won't give me a very good look at it, but I'm pretty sure."

"The one just right of center," she marveled. "I never thought *that* one would be the first, did you?"

"To tell you the truth," I replied, "I've been itching so terribly that I haven't given the matter a great deal of thought."

"The one just right of center was his *third* tooth. His *first* tooth was that upper almost in the middle, remember?"

I said that on account of my poison ivy I was having trouble remembering anything.

"What a shame," she sympathized. "And you *are* remembering his vitamins, aren't you?"

"Sure," I lied. "You know me." Well, it wasn't altogether a lie, either, because I did remember the vitamins now and then.

"Let me speak to him," she said.

I handed the instrument to Teddy, who was still at the stage where he preferred to listen, rather than do much talking, over the phone. I could hear only one side of the conversation, and it was laconic to the point of rudeness.

"Hi . . . Yes . . . Yes . . . Okay . . . All right . . . Yes . . . Fine . . . It's loose . . . No . . . Fifty cents? . . . Yes . . ."

And so the conversation proceeded, with many long pauses. The fifty cents, I deduced, was what the present-day Good Angel—you can't talk about Good Fairies any more without getting a titter, even around children—would be called upon to cough up. It seemed a ridiculous extravagance to me, since Teddy still didn't know the difference between the buying power of a penny and a million dollars.

Then, apropos of nothing, the little beast suddenly blurted out a whole, upsetting sentence:

"Those mean children," he said in an utterly casual voice which contained neither humor nor rancor, "held me down all day, and made me eat rat poison."

I heard a distinct shriek, emanating from Dixie. Teddy cringed, and held the telephone away from his ear.

"They all sat on me, and they made me eat it until I was

almost dead," he volunteered.

There was a second shriek, and he cringed again. Then he listened for a moment, and solemnly handed the phone to me. Butter wouldn't have melted in his mouth.

"Mama says she wants to talk to you," he said innocently.

"Why, *Teddy,*" I gasped, really shaken by the facility with which he had rattled off such preposterous accusations of aggravated assault and attempted murder, "you know that is a bald-faced lie! What are you, a Bad Seed or something?"

"Maybe," he agreed.

"How *could* you tell Mama that?"

He shrugged his shoulders.

"Those children have been perfectly wonderful to you. They've taken you everyplace with them, and watched out for you. Haven't they?"

"Maybe."

"Do you want to worry your mama to *death?*"

"Maybe I want my mama to come *here.*" He wiggled his tooth with his tongue.

Mary heard most of the conversation, so I didn't have too much trouble convincing her that no juvenile delinquents were really trying to kill her darling.

She talked with Ted again for awhile, and then with me. I promised I'd be sure to airmail her his tooth, if it came out, and I also was forced to agree that I hadn't set a very good example—and should be ashamed of myself—when I contracted poison ivy. She said she certainly was looking forward to seeing both of us, though, when we came home.

After I hung up, I questioned Ted some more about the rat poison, but I still don't know where he got the idea— whether is was suggested by something he had seen on television, or whether he had overheard a lurid conversation. Certainly the other children had gone out of their way to mother him, especially while I was down with the itch. It's not much of a treat for twelve and fourteen-year-olds to allow a boy his age to tag along. They had not only allowed it, but encouraged it, and took him swimming several times a day, and let him horn into their games.

And the thanks they got was a murder rap! Well, I hope this will set the record straight.

During the remaining time at Nantucket, Teddy spent most of the daylight hours with the other children. Actually, I didn't see much of him, except to give him his vitamins now and then, when I remembered them. There were so many uncles around that he sometimes got mixed up and called me Uncle Daddy. His Aunt Anne—who along with his grandmother, his Aunt Dorothy, and his Aunt Irene acted as his nurse—became Aunt You Know, because she kept asking him what her name was, and he kept pointing out that she certainly ought to know the answer, if anyone did.

Aside from the rat poison, he gave me only one other bad moment, during the whole stay. It occurred just a couple of days before we left for Charleston.

We were having lunch at The Shoe when Teddy came in from a swim. He wandered over to the table to see what we were eating, and then made a fierce face at one of his female cousins, who is almost old enough to be his mother.

"I'm going," he told her, "to knock you up!"

She blushed, tittered, and then made a lame recovery by asking no one in particular, "What does that mean?"

His Aunt You Know made an embarrassing situation worse by imitating his "Whaaat?"

And his grandmother blinked, and addressed herself to me.

"Good gracious," she remarked, "what did he say?"

"I didn't quite catch it either," I hastened to assure her. I vowed privately that I'd draw and quarter whoever had taught him language like that. I surely couldn't blame *that* on television. And I wondered what Mary would think of my family, if I brought him home spouting obscenities.

"I said," Teddy repeated, "I'm going . . ."

"Never mind," I interrupted loudly and firmly.

"to knock you up!" he finished anyway.

"Precocious, isn't he?" giggled Aunt You Know. "Is that the kind of language you teach him in Charleston?"

I couldn't help laughing, too, and so did everyone else at the table, except my mother. As I mentioned, I'm never sure just how much of the vulgar slang of the day she understands. But in this case, she gave me a very definite look of disapproval.

Teddy put up his fists, made another fierce face, and started shuffling from foot to foot. Occasionally he'd bob and weave, and snort belligerently.

"Those boys are teaching me how to box," he said. "Come on, Daddy, let's fight. I'm going to knock you up, and beat you down."

Mother waited patiently until both he and the laughter had subsided. Then she asserted quietly:

"What you are trying to say, Teddy dear, is that you intend to knock your Daddy *down* and beat him *up*—not the other way around. And if you need any help, honey, call on me!"

So a couple of days later, our vacations over, Teddy and I arrived again at Idlewild Airport in New York, to change planes for Charleston. He had a grand tan, and you could tell he had gained a few pounds. It goes without saying that he was sucking on a mint the stewardess had given him.

It was another hot day in Gotham, and people kept pushing us aside and crowding in front of us at the ticket counter. When we finally got waited on, we were told the Charleston plane would be an hour or so late.

"I want to go to the bathroom," said Teddy.

"All right."

"Right now."

"Okay. Okay."

"I'm in a hurry."

We trotted double-quick into the same rest room we had visited before. But instead of using the facilities, Teddy made a beeline for the drying machine. He studied it for a moment, and then made up his mind. He slowly put his hand on the knob and pushed it.

The machine sighed, and exhaled its fetid breath.

"Whoosh," said the machine.

"Whoosh," answered Teddy, grinning happily and mighty proud that he wasn't afraid any more. "Whoosh, eh Daddy?"

"That's my boy!" I told him.

Then he put his sticky hands in front of the monster's gaping mouth, and rubbed them briskly, in circular fashion, like a banker negotiating a fat loan.

CHAPTER 9

RED SHOES

WHEN WE GOT BACK TO CHARLESTON BOTH MARY AND THE nurse made a big fuss over Teddy, and he spent a good deal of time describing to them, with extravagant gestures, how Bonnie, the dog, chased but never caught rabbits; how James, the cat, had a tongue that was rough as sandpaper; and how Teddy, the boy, had voluntarily put his head way down deep under the salt water. That last was straight fiction, by the way, since he didn't like to get even his chest wet.

Also, perhaps encouraged by skillful pumping, he played the role of tattletale tit, and kept me on the defensive. I could have parried his thrusts if he had stuck to the truth, but his urge to be the center of attention led him to a series of lurid falsehoods.

"I'm sure, Teddy," his nurse observed cagily that night at supper, "that your daddy always gave you nice cold cereal and fruit before you went to bed."

"Nice cold cereal!" he said contemptuously. "I et hot dogs and mustard. I cooked the hot dogs myself, because Daddy wasn't ever around."

"Hot dogs?" repeated the nurse, so as to be sure that Mary was listening. "Why, Teddy, how can you be such a storyteller? What do you know about hot dogs?"

"Everything," he said darkly, hamming it up.

"You never had a hot dog in your life," Mary put in.

"The heck I didn't, eh Daddy? At Nantucket. I et *plenty*."

"Well, sure, you might have had a taste of one," I agreed. "But only after you had had your vitamins. Why don't you tell Mama about how *early* you and I went to bed every night."

"A *taste* of one!" he ridiculed me. "About all we ever had was hot dogs." He held up three fingers. "I et this many hot dogs at one time, Mama. Seven!"

"You had *seven* hot dogs for dinner?" his nurse inquired, glaring at me. "Why Teddy, you never!"

"No," he corrected her, "for breakfast."

"Oh, Lord," I said. "You don't believe *that* do you?"

"For dinner," he continued, "I et lobster and beer."

Then there was another time, a day or so later, when he overheard me ask Mary if she wanted a drink before supper.

"In Nantucket," he volunteered, "Daddy *always* had cocktails before supper. So did everybody but Granddear and me."

"Not always," I corrected him. "And so what? I was on vacation, wasn't I?"

"Always," he insisted.

"Sing, you little stool pigeon you," I dared him, showing him the back of my hand.

He held up three fingers again. "Daddy drank nine!"

I was glad Mary knew that Teddy was still an unreliable counter. He understood what two meant, but he wasn't entirely sure about any number higher than that. So when he wanted to convey the meaning of three, he sometimes said, "Two and another one." It reminded me of that wheeze about the zoo keeper who didn't know the plural of mongoose, but who ordered a couple of them by writing a letter saying, "Please send me a mongoose. P. S.: Please send another."

For a couple of weeks after our return, Teddy also invoked a purely imaginary version of Nantucket rules of conduct as a yardstick of how he intended to deport himself in Charleston.

"Granddear says," he told Mary, "that I don't *have* to wear no pants at the table. She says when you eat it's just too damned hot for pants."

"Now Teddy," I reproved him for Mary's benefit, because I didn't want her to get the idea that when my family was all by itself we sat around in our BVDs, "you know very well Granddear never said that. And she never said 'damned' in her life—and neither should you."

"I think she did," he assured us blandly. "She *certainly* did."

"My Aunt You Know," he told Mary another time, "says I don't have to go to bed until everyone else goes to bed."

"Why Teddy!" I objected for the twentieth time, "how can you tell such whoppers? Mercy me and by the great horn spoon!"

Perhaps it was a temptation for Mary to reply that she didn't care *what* his Aunt You Know—or his Granddear either—had told him. But she was tactful enough to resist it.

And even though Teddy kept describing Nantucket as a glamorous place where the lid was off insofar as restrictive rules were concerned, you could tell he was mighty glad to be home.

"My nurse is going to feed me and not *nobody* else," he'd say. "She's *my* nurse."

There was no doubt that he reveled in being the center of attention again, instead of just one of a group of children. And that meant there was also no doubt that he needed some more preparation, before the new baby came.

So Mary and I decided that autumn to send him to kindergarten, although at four-and-a-half he was still a little young for it. We felt sure that he would benefit from still more association with other children. And we knew that a little classroom discipline wouldn't hurt him in the least, either.

For my part, the decision was reached reluctantly. I suppose that when a father gets my age, he's apt to over-sentimentalize every milestone on what Thackeray describes as life's downhill journey.

But it really *is* an historic—not to mention poignant—occasion when you send your son to school for the first time. Perhaps I let myself dwell on it too much.

Of course I felt gratified that Teddy was growing up, and was *ready* to take such an important step. I knew, also, that things would be much more placid around the house in his absence—a move in the right direction.

Still, I couldn't quite forget—and here was the old sentimentalist at work again—that school signals the end of the family itself.

You can't have it otherwise, and you wouldn't if you could: But on the first day of school the family dies just a little bit.

From that day on, the members will be together less and less, until the time comes when the long-discarded toys, the tennis racket, and the college pennants are cleared out of a certain bedroom, and *his* room becomes the guest room.

You'll tell him, then, that there'll always be a place for him, if he should ever want to come back and stay. But you know he never will, and so does he.

Ah, well! As Teddy remarked the other day with a loud sigh, "It's one heck of a life."

Still, it *does* give you the blues to watch a young child take a deep breath, crawl into the protective shell of an utterly blank expression, and enter a school building for the first time. The front steps of a school are the last mile for guilelessness, and the child immediately senses it.

And just as college is youth's last stand, so is kindergarten the last hurrah for infancy. Gone forever after is the grand illusion that the world is composed entirely of people who stand ready to comfort, admire, succor, and love.

Within a span of a few moments, a child must step from an environment where adults are interested in keeping him happy and secure, to one where children are interested in keeping him unhappy and insecure.

It is a hard transition for any child, and especially for a boy.

I don't believe any female, old or young, realizes what a boy goes through every day, and as a matter of routine, during the first seven or eight grades of school. Time after time, he has to make up his mind whether to grovel or take a beating. And unless he's immune to pain, he lives in the shadow of it.

Few men write honestly about their boyhood. Perhaps,

even after they're grown, they think it would be unmanly to whine that it was often downright terrifying.

But the truth is that, compared to boyhood, war itself is a picnic. In war, there is at least the warm satisfaction of fighting shoulder-to-shoulder with comrades; whereas in school it is every lonesome individual against the cruel pack.

In Teddy's case, I was particularly concerned about a pair of sissified red sandals which Mary bought him especially for kindergarten. I felt sure that they'd cause him trouble. And I couldn't forget the reception I got in Providence, when I arrived at public school—after a few grades at a largely female day school—wearing one of those stiff collars and flowing red ties that I've already mentioned.

"The other boys are going to give him a fit, if you dress him like a girl," I warned Mary.

"But he looks so *cute,*" she reasoned. "Besides, they're boys' shoes. What do you want him to wear, hiking boots?"

"Listen, I know all about boys," I said. "They'll take his shoes away from him and tear him apart."

"If they lay a hand on him," Mary replied darkly, "you'll go have a talk with their fathers and straighten them out in a hurry."

"Oh, sure," I agreed unenthusiastically. "But, just the same, don't you think it would be better to get him a different pair of shoes?"

"No. Those go so nicely with his rompers."

"You're not going to send him to school wearing *rompers?*

What color?"

"Pink."

"He won't even come home *alive* if you send him to school in pink rompers," I predicted.

"He's four-and-a-half," she pointed out. "What should he wear to school—a charcoal gray business suit?"

"Anything but pink rompers and red shoes! Something like a pair of blue jeans and a polo shirt."

"He's only a little boy once. He'll have plently of time to wear things like that when he grows up."

"If he lives long enough to grow up!" I warned.

I suppose that somehow or other I had mixed up in my mind the tough older boys of my youth, with the present-day kindergarten set. So I was agreeably surprised, when the station wagon arrived for Teddy, to find several other pairs of rompers among the inmates. Also, instead of towering over him and talking in rough voices that were beginning to change, the other kindergarten boys were tykes about his size. I was glad to see that none of them needed a shave, either.

The station wagon was packed, and Teddy was reluctant to get in. One of the boys was crying silently, in the back seat.

"Hello there, children," I said with forced geniality, as I opened a door. "My name is Mr. Gilbreth, and this is my son, Teddy. Now you boys move over, and make room for him there on the seat. Hop in, Ted."

There wasn't so much as an answering smile—just blank stares. So I guess they were all pretty nervous. I reached over and patted the head of the boy who was crying, but he didn't take his face out of his hands.

"Get in, laddie," I told Ted.

He had on a blank stare, too. The boys hadn't moved over for him, but he got in anyway, and jammed himself into the seat.

"So long, Boy Friend," I gulped. And then I wished I hadn't called him that. But nobody seemed to notice it, least of all Ted.

So I closed the door, after making certain there were no fingers in it, and waved as the station wagon pulled away. But no one waved back.

As I had predicted, too, the red sandals *did* cause trouble. I may have been way off base about the rompers, and of course there weren't any tough, teen-aged bullies in kindergarten. But I wasn't altogether wrong about boys in general, of any age.

"Those boys," Teddy told me a few days later, "said these are *girls'* shoes."

"Well, so what?" I tried to make light of it, because he had never before paid much attention to the difference between boys and girls, and he certainly had never attached any stigma to girls' possessions.

"I don't know. But they were mean to me."

"Well, I certainly don't like that! What did they do?"

"They said these were girls' shoes."

"Yes, you told me that. And what did you do?"

"I said they were boys' shoes."

"And what did they do?"

"They said they were girls' shoes."

It sounded like a stalemate, but I wanted to be sure.

"Did they try to take them away from you?"

"No. But a fat boy pushed me down, and everybody laughed at me."

"Never mind, pal," I gulped again, "I'll get you a new pair of shoes. I suppose there'll *always* be fat boys in this world, who go around pushing people . . ."

"And then I got up and pushed him down and sat on his fat old stomach, and everybody laughed at *him,*" Teddy interrupted.

"So what about the shoes?"

"And after that, nobody didn't say they were girl's shoes no more," he gloated.

"Good boy, Teddy!" I gloated, too. And for some reason I felt mighty proud that he had excelled at the very sort of activity which I deplored.

"I did pretty good," he agreed with his customary immodesty.

"Do you like kindergarten?"

"I think I like it pretty good," he nodded. "I like it *splendid.*"

CHAPTER 10

THE STRAWBERRY

I GUESS ALMOST EVERYONE AGREES THAT OVERLY CLEVER names for boats, inns, cottages, automobiles, animals, and raisins are a sickening abomination. Even so, in my family we seem to have a penchant for this bad habit, which has been handed down to subsequent generations.

Teddy's private vocabulary is a case at point, and so are two of the cottages at Nantucket. As I've mentioned, Mother's is named The Shoe—a play on the fecund old nursery-rhyme lady who lived in one. And Dan's is the Summer Salt, a pun which he blames on his young sons.

Also, when I was about nine or ten years old, I was clever enough to name our family magazine *The Ambidextrous,* because all hands contributed to it. We issued the magazine several times a year, and circulated it round robin to the relatives. I have been told lately by one of my older sisters, whose memory is less keen than mine, that it was she not I who named the magazine. She also insisted—and this shows you how an older woman's mind can start playing tricks on her—that when I was nine or ten years old I wouldn't have known an ambidextrous from a ukelele. But no matter. It is still a pretty cloyingly cute name, regardless of who gets the credit.

The Ambi contained, among other things, a classified-ad column and a series of Lincoln-Steffansish muckrakes on such subjects as who was shirking his dishwashing chores, and who fudged regularly on taking baths. My father was the main contributor to the classified columns, bringing down the house with such racy chestnuts as, "For Sale, a bureau by a poor old man without any drawers."

My father also attempted to monopolize other departments of the magazine by inserting, *Congressional Record* fashion, every dull and technical speech either he or my mother made. When the magazine editors finally drew the line, and clipped rejection slips to his speeches, he went into a pet and started a rival family magazine. He named this the *Bimanufiabilitous,* a coined word which was supposed to indicate that two hands

—as distinguished from *The Ambidextrous'* "all hands"—contributed to it.

What I'm edging up to is that Teddy proved himself to be a chip off the old block: That autumn, at the age of four-and-a-half and in his first week at kindergarten, he managed to name the school newspaper. He thought up the name without any help from me or anyone else. In fact the name just seemed to come to him in a flash.

Teddy's school is an excellent one. The patient and dedicated woman who runs it does her best to stress the importance of striving for God, for country, and for kindergarten. School opens with a prayer, and the children then salute the American flag and sing "My Country 'Tis of Thee," "Dixie," and "Good Morning, Dear Teacher," in high shrieks. After that, there are classroom recitations and fighting in the playground.

In order to emphasize the meaning of democracy in government, this earnest and competent headmistress allows democracy of a sort to prevail within the school itself. Of course you can't have a kindergarten—any more than you could have a madhouse—that is run by its inmates. But, with a proper checkrein, you can have a kindergarten that seems to be run by its inmates.

Teddy's teacher is quite skillful at this. Whenever she feels sure she has the necessary votes in her pocket—or at any rate can corral them—she makes a great show of calling for a referendum, and allowing the majority to rule.

"Now children, you see?" she then sometimes asks. "That's how a democracy works, and that's what our country is—a democracy."

Three or four days after kindergarten opened, she spent half an hour or so telling Teddy's class that she thought a school newspaper—a by-weekly mimeographed sheet of kindergarten activities—would be of great value to them, their parents, and presumably to posterity.

She called for comments on this proposal, so as to gauge the tenor of opinion. And when it seemed obvious that the boys and girls were sold on the merits of such a publication, she called for a vote.

"All those who want us to have a kindergarten newspaper," she said, "please raise their hands."

Just about all those who were listening raised their hands.

"Excellent," she said. "That was called a vote. And if most of you *hadn't* raised your hands, then there wouldn't be a newspaper. Do you understand? The motion is carried, and the majority rules."

It was time for a cookie break, but a few minutes later she buckled down again to the task at hand.

"Now, boys and girls, we have voted to have a kindergarten newspaper. And the next question is what we should name it. I think something like *The Journal,* or *The News,* or *The Ledger,* don't you?"

She waited a moment to make sure that she still had the situation well in hand. Failing to detect any signs of mutiny, she deemed it safe to inquire, "Are there any other suggestions?"

And when there weren't any, she decided to press her luck.

"I don't want you to think that you always have to vote for *my* ideas," she said. "Maybe some of you have even *better* ideas. And if you do, I don't want you to hesitate to speak right up."

She paused again, and still nobody said anything.

"Very well, then," she continued, "if there are no other nominations . . ."

"What," blurted out Teddy, and it was the first word he had volunteered in class, "about *The Strawberry?*"

There was a general murmur of approval from his colleagues.

"What was that?" stalled the teacher. "Did you say something, Teddy?"

"Yes," he blushed, wishing he hadn't.

"Stand up, honey, when you make a nomination."

He stood up, and looked at the floor.

"Now what was your nomination?"

"The Strawberry," he whispered.

"Now you see, children," she said, deciding to make the best of the situation, "that's how you make a nomination. Very good, Teddy. And *The Strawberry* is certainly an *interesting* name, dear. But why *The Strawberry?*"

Somebody giggled, and Teddy squirmed a little. "I don't

know," he conceded, and started to sit down.

"No, stand up for just a little bit more, Teddy," she said, hoping to help him overcome his self-consciousness. "I think you did splendidly to think up a name. But a strawberry is a fruit, honey. And we're naming a newspaper, aren't we?"

Teddy didn't deny it.

"So why, dear," she bore down, "should we name a newspaper for a fruit?"

"I don't know," he repeated. Then, to hide his embarrassment, he tried to make light of it. "You can search me."

"Well why *The Journal?*" one of the older children came suddenly to his rescue.

"Or why *The News?*" asked another.

The teacher began an explanation which, she realized as she went along, was in a hopeless cause. Luckily, she has a sense of humor, so she didn't become upset, or try to use her veto power. And when her explanation was cut short by an all-but-unanimous kindergarten equivalent of a call for the question, she yielded gracefully and put the matter to a vote.

Teddy's proposal won in a walk. I found out about it— and his teacher subsequently confirmed and amplified it— when he brought home Vol. 1 No. 1 of *The Kindergarten Strawberry,* containing a front page box crediting Edward Manigault (Teddy) Gilbreth with naming the newspaper.

CHAPTER 11

THE OLD RED ROOSTER

LATE THAT AUTUMN, I WAS LUCKY ENOUGH TO BE ON HAND
at the exact moment when Teddy found he had a sense of
humor. I say that it was luck, and it was; but a certain amount
of patience was also involved, or I might not have recognized
what I had observed.

The middle-aged father, as a general rule, has both the
time and the temperament for such observation. Unlike a

younger man, he is no longer driven by too much ambition. If he hasn't set the world on fire, at least he has developed a philosophy not to waste matches on things he *knows* won't burn.

So he is attuned and receptive to the pastime of Children Watching. And he is now sufficiently cynical to enjoy the wriest joke of all: The portrayal, in bright-eyed miniature, of his own sagging image.

I suppose there must be some definite juncture in the life of *every* child, when the heady realization occurs that it is possible to make other people laugh and to disguise his own true-life personality by posing as a clown.

The Pagliacci at our house hadn't meant to be funny when he named *The Strawberry*. Quite the opposite. But it was about a month after that incident when he *did* emerge as a premeditated juvenile humorist with a repetitious repertoire containing one lone joke.

It should be borne in mind that the age of four is a time for endless memorizing. A child begins to learn to count, to say parts of the alphabet, and to recite various nursery rhymes and other nonsense. His vocabulary grows, and his power of retention soon becomes as acute as it will ever be, in his lifetime.

When Teddy started to parrot a whole boring series of endless recitations, I couldn't resist teasing him occasionally, by mixing him up. I'll admit that it was probably bad psychology, and certainly was picking on someone who isn't my size. But the mind of a memorizing child is so intense, so literal, and so precise that the temptation was strong to confuse him momentarily, in order that I could enjoy his utter, indignant exasperation.

About the first thing he ever committed to rote was a portion of *The Night Before Christmas*. He had accomplished this the preceding December, when he was still three years old. But ten or eleven months later, with the frost upon the pumpkin, he was still reciting it whenever he could find anyone willing to listen.

So, to get a rise out of him, I would sometimes go around the house improvising rhymes and lisping:

" 'Twas the night before Thanksgiving, when all through the shanty, not a creature was stirring, not even old Santy. The . . ."

"No, you're all mixed up, Daddy," he would complain impatiently. "You haven't got it straight."

"I have too," I'd tell him. "What do you think I am, stupid or something? 'Twas the day before Easter, when all through the peninsulas, not a creature was stirring, not even Good King Wenceslaus."

"No! No! 'Twas the *night* before *Christmas,* when all through the *house,* not a creature . . ."

"Not a creature was stirring," I continued, "not even a spouse."

"No, Daddy! Listen. Please! Not even a mouse."

"The shoes had been hung by the fireside with caution,"

I chanted sadistically, oblivious to the corrections, "all set
for Santa's annual extortion . . ."

"Daddy," he shouted, all but livid with frustration, "you
must be sick. You're *all mixed up!"*

Another poem he soon memorized was that doggerel
which begins, "One, two, button my shoe," and ends, "Nine,
ten, a big fat hen."

He was so proud of this achievement that he made a fili-
buster of it. And since we had praised him when he first
mastered the verse, he expected our laudatory comments to
continue every time he gave the vocal marathon another
milking.

Then Pagliacci emerged as full-blown—if that is the
phrase I want—as Botticelli's half-shell Venus. At the time,
I was trying to read in the living room, and Teddy was standing right in front of my chair. He was reciting, over and over
again and in a monotone a few decibals below bedlam, what
had become his favorite ode:

". . . Five, six," he intoned, "pick up *sticks.* Seven, eight,
lay them straight. Nine, ten, a *big* fat . . ."

There was a break in the deafening rhythm, and I looked
up just in time to see a sly gleam come into his eyes. He
pressed his lips together tightly, as he lengthened the pause
for dramatic effect.

Then he clasped his hands behind him, and rocked back
on his heels in preparation for his first buffola.

"Seven, eight, lay them straight," he repeated, so as to

make certain that I had heard him properly, that I was properly backgrounded, and that I wouldn't miss the forthcoming punchline. "Nine, ten, a big fat . . . a big fat *rooster.*"

Mary came into the room just as he got to the "rooster," a word which he actually squealed, so delighted was he with his own wit. Then he exploded into deep, uncontrollable laughter which left him lying limp and wheezing on the rug.

We couldn't help roaring, too. In fact his intentional mixup, patterned after mine, all but panicked his audience —so much so that his nurse arrived on the run to see what the commotion was.

"A big fat rooster," Teddy managed to squeak breathlessly for her benefit, thus bringing down the house again. So we three adults ended up just about as limp as he was. And every time we'd look at him, rolling there on the rug in paroxysms of self-satisfied delight, we'd start laughing all over again.

Certainly he couldn't have asked for a more responsive audience. And he was so flushed with his initial success at humor that he kept repeating, every time he could get his breath:

"A big fat *rooster.*"

This repetition went on for days thereafter. And if I absentmindedly forgot to give a hearty laugh each time, Teddy would pull at my sleeve, and shout:

"A big fat rooster, eh Daddy? Do you hear me?"

After some weeks of this, even he began to perceive that

the jest was wearing a bit thin. So he started to use "rooster" as a mixup word in various sentences.

"Please pass the rooster," he'd say at the breakfast table, when he wanted the butter. "Mama's going to have a little rooster," he'd chortle whenever the subject of the new baby came up.

And, again, every time he used the word he confidently expected to roll 'em in the aisles. Occasionally he succeeded, too, which served only to spur him on to new and occasionally embarrassing extremes.

"Yonder comes Dr. Rooster," he shouted out the window one evening, when his pediatrician came to call. And although Mary tried to hush him, he repeated the same greeting in the front hall. I certainly should have had better manners, but I couldn't help snickering—and a surprised and slightly indignant look passed over the doctor's face momentarily. Of course, like every ham, Teddy laughed the loudest at his own joke—and then repeated it, so that everyone could enjoy it for a third time. By then, the pediatrician, who is a good sport, was chuckling too.

A couple of days later, Teddy and I were passing the time of day at a filling station down the road from our house. Our gas tank had been filled, and we were sitting with a group of loungers on one of the islands where the gas pumps are. Business was slack, and I was catching up on such neighborhood news as who had recently outfoxed the game warden, and where the new four-lane highway would be built. There aren't any cracker-barrels in filling stations, but they manage to fill the vacuum left when drugstores and supermarkets killed the general store.

During a lull in the conversation, one of the filling-station employees turned to Teddy.

"Well, Bubba," he asked, "is your red-headed old daddy behaving hisself pretty well these days?" He slipped Teddy the remaining half of a package of gumdrops. And my son plopped two of them in his mouth, and hid the rest behind his back where he didn't think I'd see them.

I suppose I should explain that, despite my years, my hair remains a rather conspicuous red. I am neither gray nor utterly bald, which some impolite and probably envious people have intimated is a pity, as any change would be for the better.

"His name isn't Old Daddy," drawled Teddy, with his mouth full. "It's Old Red Rooster. Oh-ho-ho-ho-ho!"

His deafening peals of merriment were, for once, equalled if not exceeded by all but one member of his audience.

And as the loose-lipped and rather uncouth merriment continued, accompanied by thigh-slappings and rib-nudging, I made a mental note to change my brand of gasoline and take my business elsewhere, if the appellation showed the slightest sign of becoming a permanent nickname.

And I also decided that it was about time to quit teasing Pagliacci.

CHAPTER 12

CANDY KID

A MYSTERY OF PARENTHOOD WHICH BEGGARS SOLUTION IS how a four-year-old child, without access to money or fudge-making recipes, can keep an apparently inexhaustible supply of sweetmeats on hand and in mouth.

At almost the same time that he discovered his sense of humor, Teddy also discovered his sense of cunning. And he devoted this new-found talent, full time, to the obtaining and concealing of candy.

Practically over night, the little wretch started to display the same sort of craftiness toward candy that an alcoholic displays toward spirits. And although his modus operandi was sly as a fox, he left behind him a sticky-fingered trail of perfidy.

I don't mean to say that our Candy Kid actually secreted Baby Ruths in the chandelier or dangled Lifesavers out of the window on a string. But almost.

Doorknobs, banister rails, drawer pulls, and especially his face betrayed him with the gooey evidence of dissipation. Mary reported that to kiss him goodnight, at that stage of the game, was tantamount in calories to the consumption of half a chocolate bar and a middle-sized helping of charlotte russe.

She and I have long been advocates of an austere diet for young boys. We believe that candy, cake, and cookies make a child weak, interfere with his appetite, bloat his stomach, and give him cavities. Or, as the Irish say, too many cookies spoil the broth.

But in spite of our strong views on the matter, Teddy became a shameless beggar—a pleading, cajoling, round-eyed suppliant—for sweets. And when candy wasn't actually given him, he managed to find it, with all the instinctive skill of a French hog locating truffles.

I've never been able to devise a defense against adults who deliberately hand candy to Teddy. I put them in the same category as salegirls who urge women to try on mink coats to see whether they fit; and pet shop owners who thrust appealing balls of live fur into children's arms, and ask them how they'd like to take home a great Dane puppy.

When handed a bag of candy, Teddy would always turn his back, crouch with stealth, and swiftly jam two or three pieces into his mouth, so as to be sure that he got in his licks before I tried to take the bag away from him.

This furtive, swift gobbling gave the impression that he didn't get enough to eat at home, that he was scared to death of me, and that he thought the donor of the candy might be an Indian giver.

I found out fairly early in the game that the phrase "like taking candy from a baby" means something just the opposite when the baby gets to be four years old.

It is humanly possible to take away what remains in Teddy's *bag* of candy. But I challenge anyone to divest him of the pieces he has jammed into his mouth. Personally, I'd just as soon put my finger in a rattrap or a beehive.

If you don't force but merely *order* him to spit out the stuff, his jaws start to work desperately, and his cheeks dimple from the pressure of swallowing. Only when the last bit of candy has been gulped will he deign to respond.

"What did you say?" he'll ask, cupping his ear so as to be sure not to miss your important words. "I didn't quite *hear* you."

The outright filching of candy by a child can perhaps be dismissed as more cute than cunning—if the victim of the theft is an acquaintance who understands children. But it's a different matter when the victim is an unsympathetic, cold-blooded corporation, such as a supermarket.

Recently, after Teddy and I had shopped at such a place, I was aghast to discover on the ride home that he was palming a partially consumed package of Charms, which I certainly had not paid for.

"Okay, Sticky Fingers," I stormed angrily, "where in the Sam Hill did you get that candy? No, don't add lying to your other vices. I want the truth. You *stole* it, didn't you?"

"Sandy Claus gave it to me," he said airily. "You want a piece, Daddy?"

"Santa Claus doesn't give anything to thieves but *ashes,*" I told him. "And you're not going to catch me eating stolen goods. From now on . . ." I gulped and winced, as I noticed that the two pockets at the top of his rompers were bulging. "Holy mackeral, boy, what have you got in *there?*"

"In where?" asked Teddy, folding his arms tightly against the pockets, like a girl who's lost the top of her bathing suit.

I pulled over to the curb, stopped, and frisked him. By that time, the remainder of the Charms had disappeared into his mouth, but I managed to retrieve about an eighty-cent assortment of mints, lollypops, chewing gum, and candy bars.

"Do you know what happens to boys who steal?" I asked furiously. "They go to jail."

"And there's no candy in jail," Teddy helped me build up the scene.

"You bet there isn't. All you get to eat is bread and water."

"And you have to eat the crusts, too, don't you, Daddy?" he added.

"You can say that again," I agreed. "Ye Gads, boy, what . . ."

"Are you going to *keep* my candy?"

"I should say not," I assured him. "If you want to be a juvenile delinquent and a thief, that's your business. But don't think you're going to make a Fagin out of me. This stuff goes back to the supermarket."

"Whaaat?" he whinnied. "Daddy, *do!* They got more than they can eat right now."

"It doesn't matter how much they've got. That's their business."

"You want to make them sick?"

"I don't care what happens to them. But I'm not going to let you steal."

"How about all those things *you* steal from them!"

"Don't talk like that!" I warned him, thankful that no one else was around to hear him trying to frame me.

"What's in those bags, then?" He pointed to the produce I had just bought.

"But I *paid* for those things, that's the difference."

"Oh."

"And you didn't, did you?" I drove home the point.

"No. Because I didn't *have* any money."

"And when you don't *have* any money, you dope," I shouted, "you can't buy anything!"

"That's no fair," he complained.

"Yes it is," I contradicted him, beginning to get angry again. "What are you, a Communist or something?"

I was tempted just to heave the candy out of the car window, and go on home. I knew that the supermarket would never miss it. But I had to teach Teddy a lesson. So we drove back there, and located the manager.

He was dressed in the uniform of the supermarket chain: A green smock bearing his name on the breast pocket, flamboyant pink shirt, black patent-leather bow tie, and silly overseas cap which matched the smock. Instead of shrinking in shame because he had to wear such humiliating apparel, he seemed to consider the uniform a badge of high office.

I introduced Teddy and myself to him, and then was forced to wait because one of his checkout girls rang a bell, and he had to hustle forward to initial a check, before she could cash it.

"My boy here," I said, trying to make light of it, "is trying to bankrupt you. He doesn't understand about money. So he took this candy without paying for it."

"He couldn't hardly bankrupt *us,* mister," the manager replied humorlessly. "We are but one of more than four thousand outlets in thirty-seven states, as well as . . ."

I was saved momentarily by the bell, which summoned the factual bore to initial another check.

"Besides," he added, when he returned, "we put aside a per cent of our profits to cover shoplifting cases like this."

"Well now, wait a minute!" I protested. "I wouldn't call this shoplifting."

"What *would* you call shoplifting, mister?"

"Dammit, he's only four years old. And besides we brought the stuff back, didn't we?"

"Are you sure you brought it *all* back, mister?"

"Of course I'm sure," I snapped.

"Do you want to pay for the goods, or leave them here?"

"I'll leave the goods here. Oh, wait a minute," I remembered, "there was one other thing. A package of Charms. I'll pay for that. He's eaten it."

"Are you sure *that's* all?"

"Positive, dammit! Do you want me to pay you, or do I have to go through a checkout line?"

He said he'd take the money, and Teddy and I got out of there. On the way home, I started to give my son a lecture about the necessity of being honest, and how you had to pay for just about everything you got on this vale of tears, and also how if you thought you could get something for nothing, you had another think coming.

"So you mustn't take no candy from the store," Teddy agreed, but with such a pronounced lisp that he obviously had something in his mouth.

"Why, Teddy," I hollered, "don't tell me that while I was talking to the manager, you stole some more candy! Open your mouth!"

Since I was driving, I had to keep my eyes on the road.

But I could see, in a momentary glance, that he was chewing and swallowing hard. Finally he opened his mouth and put out his tongue, which was raspberry red.

"It's empty, mister," he assured me. "See?"

Ever since then, I've made it a practice to frisk him thoroughly before passing through the checkout counters. So far, his pockets and hands have been empty, but sometimes not his mouth.

As things stand now, I'm open to suggestions. Apparently, there's no way to make him quit the stuff unless he wants to quit it. And, believe me, he doesn't want to.

CHAPTER 13

FAST FREIGHT

NOT FAR FROM CHARLESTON, THERE IS A STRETCH OF BLACK-
top highway where a railroad track comes right up next to
the road and parallels it for fifteen or twenty miles.

Teddy and I were out driving one afternoon a few weeks
before Christmas, when we gradually began to overtake a
northbound freight on this stretch of track. The occasion
turned out to be another one of those steps away from in-

121

nocence, with worldly wisdom taking the place of ingenu-
ousness.

We were cruising along at about fifty-five miles an hour.
Teddy had seen trains before, but only at a distance, or
gliding into and out of stations. But to see one up close,
clanking over the rails like a red streak half-a-mile long, was
a new and miraculous experience.

At first, as we pulled up even with the caboose, the boy
held his breath and grabbed my shoulder for reassurance.
The caboose was swaying and sucking up dust, as it ram-
rodded along, and the whole train was making a fearful
racket.

"She won't scare," he said hopefully, falling back again
on a phrase which for some reason invariably ascribed the
female gender to danger.

After a moment or two, when he saw that there was no
apparent harm in the red monster and that his dead-game
old daddy was bravely unafraid, he relaxed his hold.

Then, as our car gradually gained on the train, passing
freight car after freight car, Teddy watched in utter wonder.
Sometimes he giggled ecstatically and sometimes he jumped
up and down on the front seat, where he had been tracking
up the upholstery.

Because we were moving at almost the same speed, it
took a few minutes before we finally overtook the diesel at
the front. An old-timer was at the throttle, not more than
thirty feet away from Teddy's perch.

As far as adults are concerned, jet planes and space travel have robbed trains of much of the enchantment they had back in the days when people talked about Going Like Sixty, instead of Breaking the Sound Barrier.

And the trains themselves, which don't spit steam any more, have surrendered a good bit of the glamor of their coal-burning predecessors. Today's diesel locomotive can no more compete with space ships than can the grizzled old Brotherhood engineers, with their greasy denim-billed caps, compete with the daring young man in the bubble-headed suits.

The locomotive engineers, most of whom date back to the days when little boys hollered choo-choo-choo instead of beep-beep-beep and A-OK, are probably quite aware that their glamor has been eclipsed.

No one cares particularly, any more, whether the 8:47 west-bound freight out of Tuxedo Junction is on time or five hours late. Boys don't line the river bank to watch the express go helling over the trestle. And folks don't set their clocks by the lonesome whistle of the Midnight Limited, as it knifes down into the gap in a cascade of sparks, with a hot-box squealing murder. In fact even the gold-plated watches of "railroad accuracy," which the conductors wore attached to chains draped across the ample blue serge vests of their uniforms, are being replaced by thin wristwatches which magically wind themselves, even underwater.

To a four-year-old, though—as I discovered on our Nantucket trip—there is nothing particularly remarkable about a plane. It starts on the ground, makes a racket and flies into the air. So what! Sparrows can do the same thing, only more gracefully and without so much fuss. So can robins and blue jays, not to mention pigeons which will eat peanuts practically out of your hand.

As for noise, thunder is louder; and when it comes to size, a house is bigger. And so is a train. A train. Oh, my!

The engineer of the train we were paralleling had on one of those billed caps I mentioned, that are still the trademark of railroad men. He noticed the four-year-old riding on the front seat. And maybe he also noticed the look on the boy's face when Teddy observed that a human being—an old man wearing steel-rimmed glasses and a cap—was guiding the red monster with as much ease and nonchalance as I drove our puny automobile.

At any rate, the engineer leaned out of his cab and waved. Teddy gasped in delight, jumped again into the air, and waved back wildly.

The engineer seemed mighty pleased about that. His face broke into a slow grin. Then he reached for something, and the diesel's whistle went wooo-wooo-woo-woo.

It wasn't the proper whistle of a steam-spitting locomotive, but I had to admit that—right up close as we were—it sounded pretty good. And Teddy thought it was first-rate.

"Oh, my!" he gasped. "Daddy, did you hear him blow the whistle for me? Oh, mercy!"

A few moments later, the tracks veered away from the highway—in the old days they would have said it was the highway which veered away from the tracks—and the train was soon out of sight. Teddy and I drove in silence for awhile. He sat down, for a change, and out of the corner of an eye I could see that he was meditating.

I knew pretty well what was going through his mind. The one thing that a boy that age wants more than anything else is to grow up. He wants to be as big and as strong as his Old Man, and to give orders to children, and to stay up as late as he pleases. And so the boy begins to become a little ashamed, occasionally, of acting *like* a boy.

In this case, he had been wildly pleased and excited, whereas the Old Man had been no more than faintly amused and calm. And I believe that Teddy imagined he had lost face with me, by being so enthusiastic.

"Well, what did you think of it?" I asked.

"Think of *what?*" he asked with studied nonchalance.

"Of the train?"

"Oh, *that,*" he dismissed it blandly as hardly worth mention. "Big son-of-a-gun, wasn't it?"

CHAPTER 14

TELEVISION NUT

FEW AWAKENINGS ARE MUCH RUDER THAN THE DISCOVERY that a man is becoming a bloody bore to his children.

The disillusioning eye opener came to me in November of that year. Up until then, Teddy had tried to monopolize every minute of my time. If I were lying down, he wanted to get in bed with me; if I were sitting, he wanted to joggle in my lap; and if I were standing, he wanted to ride on my shoulders. Since practice is supposed to make perfect, I should have been Olympic material at Pease Porridge Hot, Pattycake, and Trot, Trot to Boston.

All of this attention was flattering. But sometimes, after a couple of hours of reading aloud or playing games of the Me-and-My-Shadow genre, I'd begin to feel hopelessly fenced in. And then the problem was to escape from Teddy's clutches without hurting his feelings.

"Oh goodness," I said on one typical occasion. "See what time it is? Look at my wristwatch! Almost four o'clock."

Since Teddy couldn't tell time, and didn't have the patience to learn, any reference to clocks or watches put him immediately on the defensive.

"Why do you say that for—that it's almost four o'clock?" he countered.

"Because I've got to run. I'm late right now. Ten minutes."

"What are you late *for?*" he asked skeptically.

"A conference. This has been fun. But I've got to run."

"Will you take me to it?"

"Take you to a conference?" I asked, as if that were the most inane request I'd ever heard. "Why, Teddy, you *know* that little boys aren't allowed to go to conferences."

Since he didn't even know what a conference was in the first place, I figured he couldn't very well prolong the discussion.

"They can't?" he surrendered with some disappointment. "Oh, dear!" Then he added, "Well, when I grow up can I go to one?"

"Go to a conference?"

"Yes. When I grow up to be seven years old, can I go to one then?"

"If you're good," I gave my standard reply.

"And if I'm *very* good," he stalled, trying to keep the fence around me for awhile longer, "I can go to *plenty* of them."

"You bet," I agreed. "Well, now I'm twelve minutes late. See what the watch says?"

"Can I hear it tick?"

"All right. Just for a second then. I've really got to run."

He put his ear to the watch, and affected rapt concentration, which continued for a minute or so, until I got restless and pulled my wrist away.

"You're twelve minutes late, all right," he agreed. "Will you be back home right after the conference?"

"I hope so."

"I guess you can go then," he agreed graciously.

Incidentally, I found out some years ago that "conference" is one of the most useful nouns in the language, not only in dealing with children but with adult nuisances as well. Few bores have the gall to make a man late for a conference. So I've just about stopped going to meetings any more. Occasionally I make a visitation or hold an audience, but usually it's a conference.

By November, though, I had noticed that if anyone in our house were having an increased number of conferences, it was Teddy. He was underfoot less and less and, although he did his best not to put my nose out of joint, he was sometimes offering lame excuses to escape from *me*.

"I'm having a grand time helping you to throw baseballs all day," he'd tell me with exaggerated enthusiasm, "but I got to go inside now."

"What for?" I'd complain. "I'm just getting warmed up. Here, see if you can field this hot grounder."

"No thanks. I got to go and rest myself, so I won't be too exhausted. I don't want to get a spitting headache, you know!"

"What are you talking about! Boys don't get exhausted."

"Gracious goodness, I'm late right now. Look at your watch. Six hours!"

After that, instead of playing hard-to-get, I guess I sometimes tried to force myself on him. But it didn't do any good, because I knew I had been eclipsed—eclipsed by a TV set.

If there were any way to sue the networks for alienation of affections and crabbing a father's act, I'd have an open-and-shut case.

Of course all children find out eventually that their fathers don't know everything. But when you bring a TV set into the house, you advance the date by a matter of years.

Because a father, however talented, suffers irreparably if compared with the various specialists on TV. Even when a fifty-year-old man prides himself on still being slim as a boy —especially if the boy is a heavy eater—he can't be expected to bat as well as Mickey Mantle. And he can't be expected to sing as well as Perry Como, fly through the air as well as Mary Martin, or follow a day-old trail as well as Lassie. And while I hope I'm not the least bit jealous of any of those people—and certainly not of a collie dog who, according to what I hear, is really nothing but a female impersonator anyway—I'm bound to admit that my vanity suffered.

I can cite chapter and verse.

For instance, there was a time when Teddy would do *anything*—even go to bed without a murmur—if I would perform my trick with a couple of oranges. I grant it isn't much of a feat, although it took years of my boyhood to perfect it. I simply juggle the two oranges in one hand.

Then one night, staying up later than he should, Teddy was watching the Ed Sullivan Show. And suddenly he started screaming, "Daddy, Daddy, come quick and look!"

Well, I came and looked, and of course it was one of those professional jugglers who starts out with twenty or thirty Indian clubs, and finally gets hats, walking sticks and various pieces of furniture into the air.

"I still think you do pretty good with two oranges, though," Teddy told me loyally, when he saw my face fall.

But just the same, I knew my trick was dead, and that in the future he'd hardly bother to look up, even if I had fruit enough to make ambrosia, flying all through the kitchen.

Some Meddlesome Matties, complaining about sex and violence, recommend that parents act as TV censors. But in order to censor shows, a parent would first have to watch them. And it certainly would be courting trouble for anyone with an adult mind to sit, night after night, through a parade of practically hopeless programs, punctuated by posturing medicine men who urge you to become a self-dosing hypochondriac, and by handsome sapheads who beg you to test-drive a new car right to the gates of the Poor-house.

Potentially, TV is more dangerous to an adult mind than to a juvenile one. And, certainly, a parent's first duty is to remain sane. Stated simply, in the language of the announcers, "A *sane* parent is a *good* parent."

There is little doubt, either, that TV sets, besides mass-producing an inferiority complex among fathers, are at the bottom of many of today's tensions. When they are in working order, they encourage idleness. And when they are broken, they must have the attention of a high-priced and usually insolent fixer, who invades the privacy of your home and then demonstrates that he is smarter than you are.

Why then have a TV set at all? Why risk turning your child into a precocious wiseacre who, instead of saying God Bless You when you sneeze, urges you to Stop Spreading Germs and to Get Blessed Relief with a five-way medicine which does the work of aspirin without upsetting your "stommick"?

Certainly in the old days everyone got along all right without TV. Back when I was a boy, the only professional entertainers who came into the house were local performers hired occasionally for children's parties—the magicians and whistlers who imitated birdcalls while their hands cast shadows purporting to be ducks, swans, and eagles. Even these artists suffered quickly from overexposure, though—usually when they were about one-quarter through their act—and were seldom asked back for a second performance.

So if we could struggle along without TV then, why not now?

The answer is discipline. The television "medium"—perhaps a flattering name for anything so far below average—is one of the greatest advancements in discipline since Alcatraz Prison.

Yes, in our effete age, TV has replaced the woodshed. And I suppose I'm as guilty as everyone else, in taking the easy way out.

"If you don't behave yourself and stop throwing knives at your baby brother this instant," parents are threatening darkly, "you can't watch tonight's thrilling installment of *I Played Russian Roulette With a Grizzly Bear, as a Secret Agent for the FBI.*"

Besides spankings, TV also has replaced milder forms of discipline. For example, there was a time when naughty children were sent to bed without any supper. That was back in the days when eating was deemed a privilege. But nowadays, instead of considering it a reward, children expect to be rewarded *for* it.

"If you don't get right back in your high chair and finish *all* your ice cream," the modern father will say, "you can't stay up and see the Late, Late Show. And don't think I'm fooling, either, because if you mess around with me you'll find, much to your regret, that I mean exactly what I say!"

In fairness, I suppose I should add that TV has also taught Teddy some useful things that I myself failed to get through his head. There was, for example, the matter of the days of the week. At first, he wasn't interested in learning their names or the order in which they fell. As far as he was concerned, a day was simply a day, and didn't need a special name of its own.

But when he became aware of TV programming, the days became all important. And he'd ask me every morning at breakfast:

"What's the name of today, Daddy?"

"What difference does it make?" I'd tease him, giving him back the same line of reasoning that he used to give me. "It's just another day."

"But what is its name?"

"I believe it's either yesterday or tomorrow—I'm not quite sure which."

"No, *Daddy*," he'd shout, shaking his head. "What's its *name*—Sunday and Thursday and all them others."

"Oh, *that* kind of name. Why didn't you say so? Today's Tuesday."

"Tuesday," he'd mumble. "Doug Edwards, Nannette Fabray, Rifleman, Three Stooges, and Wyatt Earp."

"And what comes after Tuesday?" I'd quiz him.

"Wednesday. Millionaire, Our Miss Brooks, and Rin Tin Tin. Then Thursday. Real McCoys, Bat Masterson, and Gail Storm. Then Friday . . ."

TV also has enlarged his vocabulary considerably, particularly when it comes to obsolete slang. The movies now being televised don't go back quite as far as "Twenty-three skiddoo" and "Oh you kid"—which was where I came in. But Teddy knows most of the fresh talk of the last thirty or forty years, ranging all the way from, "Not this baby" to "So's your old man." And when he likes the way things are going, he sometimes turns back the clock a mere fifteen years, and enthuses, "Hubba-hubba!"

Also, he is an authority on the esoteric language of Prohibition-era gangsters.

"I'm stir crazy, and I'm going to take you for a ride and rub you out with a pineapple," he snarled from the corner of his mouth one evening, after sitting enraptured through a George Raft movie. Then he took a fifty-cent piece, which he had borrowed from the top of my bureau, and flipped it nonchalantly up into the air. He didn't catch it, though.

I'll have to stand up for TV, however, against critics who accuse it of teaching ruthlessness. Children don't need lessons in that subject. Besides, as the TV spokesmen are quick to point out, the programs aren't as ruthless as the old nursery rhymes and bedtime stories.

I don't believe any TV writer would dare to go as far as the author of *Tattletale Tit* who, if you remember, recommended that his protagonist's tongue be split and fed piecemeal to every dog in town. Certainly being encased in concrete and dropped in the river—the customary fate of squealers in the gangster shows on TV—is more humane than that!

Then in *Goosey Goosey Gander*—which children today probably think has something to do with prodding an airport town in Newfoundland—a poor old man is hurled bodily down a flight of stairs for failing to say his prayers. Not a very good example of freedom of religion!

And in *Jack and the Beanstalk,* the frightened lad in the title role is threatened with having his bones ground into sandwich spread, simply because his blood smells like that of an Englishman.

Also, there are any number of bedtimes stories, such as *Little Red Riding Hood,* where the prospect of being eaten alive by wild animals is dangled with gleeful suspense.

As for the televised horror shows, children soon get sated, and then become more bored than horrified. I remember that I practically went into shock, when as a child I first saw a movie in which vampires went around in opera capes and sucked blood out of people. Today, what with green-faced werewolves from outer-space, vampires are tame stuff.

"Does that sneaky-looking man have tired blood—is that why he's looking for new blood all the time?" Teddy inquired with blasé curiosity after watching a reel or so of *Dracula*. "Why doesn't he wear a coat with sleeves in it? And why in the world doesn't he leave that woman alone, and ask the Red Cross for help from the Blood Bank, eh Daddy?"

He also was more annoyed than thrilled by *King Kong*, and kept remarking that the leading lady, Miss Fay Wray, was "just too darn noisy for me!"

I was in college when I first saw *King Kong*, and even though I was a full-grown youth I'm bound to say that her screams scared me so that I all but held my ears. If they ever give an Oscar for screaming, Miss Wray should still lead the field by a whoop and a holler.

She certainly had adequate cause to yell, too. After all, she *was* being clutched in the hand of a giant gorilla, presumably bent on deflowering her, who as I remember was climbing the outside of a New York skyscraper oblivious to streams of machine-gun bullets fired from hastily summoned aircraft.

In *King Kong* they had everything except a forest fire, but the picture didn't impress Teddy.

"Well, you'll have to admit," I said when the show was over, "that King Kong himself was fierce."

"He looked more like a big toy than a live monkey," Teddy said knowingly. "And that poor woman is *sick*. She needs something to Calm Jittery Nerves. What's on the other channel, Daddy?"

CHAPTER 15

TELLING TIME

BECAUSE OF TELEVISION, TEDDY BECAME OBSESSED THAT autumn with punctuality. Nothing irritated him more than to be late for one of his favorite programs like *The Four Roosters,* which was his mixup appellation—still expected to cause hysterics—for *The Three Stooges.*

Yet, despite his compulsion to be on time, I couldn't get him interested in learning to tell time. Instead, he preferred to make a nuisance of himself by continually asking other people. And if it turned out that he was late for one of his programs, he unhesitatingly placed the onus on his informant.

"Two minutes *past* seven!" he'd repeat in injured tones, as if such tardiness were a heavy cross for one so young to bear. "Gracious peace, see what you done? You made me two minutes late for *Lassie*."

Then, still pouting, he'd rush for the TV set, twist the switch, and tap his foot impatiently until the machine warmed up and the picture came on.

To make matters worse, some members of the household —those who can't bear to see him disappointed in anything —began to volunteer time-checks every few minutes. And when he was late, they'd race to the TV set ahead of him, and get it warmed up in advance.

All of this became increasingly annoying to me. It seemed pretty plain that, unless I put my foot down, Teddy's TV schedule would become the tail which wagged the whole family.

My best hope was to try again to teach him to tell time. So, even though it was an act of extravagance, I bought him a wristwatch. I figured that, once he owned his own timepiece, he'd make a new effort to read it.

But although he wound and set his watch practically continuously, he still wouldn't learn. The only change caused by my purchase was that instead of asking, "What time it is?" he now inquired, "What time it is *on my watch?*" Then he would push into your face, with all the vigor of an automobile salesman trying to light your cigarette, a bony and usually

grimy wrist. Since his watch was always set haphazardly—
on something that might have been Greenwich Mean or
Tokyo Time, but certainly wasn't local—you'd have to
wrestle his wrist aside before you could look elsewhere and
tell him. Then he'd complain about that, as well as being
late for one of his programs.

In spite of his attitude, I spent quite a few hours trying
to show him what the big hand said and what the little hand
said. In so doing, I discovered that it is all but impossible
to talk about time-telling without automatically rotating your
arms around your head—just as a man will start making cir-
cles in the air with his finger when you ask him to define a
spiral. And sometimes Teddy would advise me to open the
windows and let in some fresh air, if I intended to do my
exercises in the house.

I looked for—but couldn't find—a "How To" book on
time-telling. Also, as I often do when problems arise involving Ted, I tried to remember how my father had handled
such a situation. But I couldn't recall a single lesson involving
a clock.

I *did* remember, though, that my father was a firm be-
liever in a system of rewards for children. For instance, when
he was teaching us short cuts in arithmetic, he'd hand out
largess in much the same way that a seal trainer distributes
fish.

"Now this one is for children under ten—and no prompting from you older morons," he'd say, enjoying immensely his role as quiz-master. "Quick, now—and I'll take only one answer. How much is fifty-six times fifty-six?"

And using one of his short cuts, we'd figure that fifty-six was thirty-one more than twenty-five and six more than fifty. Then squaring the six, which gave you thirty-six, you'd come up with the answer of thirty-one, thirty-six, or three thousand, one hundred and thirty-six.

"Right," my father would crow, handing a chocolate bar, from a large wholesale carton, to the child who had given the answer first. "All right, now here's a question for all children under seven—and no prompting, *please!*"

These days, because of inflation, you can't get much mileage out of a chocolate bar. However, the reward system is still sound enough, I believe. But you have to increase the ante. There was a time, for instance, when a father would promise his son a gold watch if he didn't smoke until his twenty-first birthday. Today some fathers promise their children convertibles if they graduate from junior high school without getting involved in a shot-gun wedding or marijuana parties. So with Christmas coming up, I decided to promise Teddy a special reward.

"Santa Claus will bring you some nice presents," I said. "But I'll go Santa one better and give you an electric train —if you can tell time by Christmas day."

What I had failed to take into account is that once you promise a child something, you are committed to it, regardless of whatever conditions you have imposed. You and the child both know that you are not going to dangle a present in front of him and then fail to deliver it—especially on Christmas.

So when it became apparent that Teddy simply wasn't going to be able to tell time by Christmas, both he and I realized that my only problem was to find a way I could deliver the unearned reward, without losing face.

The most obvious face saver in such a situation is for the father to make believe that he has forgotten all about the strings attached to the present. Then, on Christmas, the present is delivered, and nothing is ever said about its being a reward.

Teddy and I were both prepared to adopt that course of action but, even so, I found I couldn't get my chestnuts out of the fire quite that easily.

Days after I had carefully avoided any reference to big hands and little hands, Mary and the nurse were still enjoying themselves by keeping the subject open.

"Don't you *want* an electric train for Christmas?" Mary would ask him. "You know you do. Well, there's only two more weeks for you to learn how to tell time."

"Your daddy," the nurse would chime in, "means *exactly* what he says, too. And if he says you're not going to get an electric train unless you learn to tell time, you're not going to *get* an electric train unless you learn to tell time. Isn't that right, Mr. Gilbreth?"

I'd glare at her, and then make believe I wasn't paying attention.

"That's right," Mary would answer for me. And I'd glare at her too, because she knew very well that I'd already bought the train, and that Teddy was certain to get it.

I don't chalk up entirely to sadism the unfortunate attitude of Mary and the nurse. It's true that on some occasions I have gently chided both of them for being too easy with Teddy, so perhaps they enjoyed putting me on the spot. But principally, I think, they wanted the train to be a delightful surprise. And the best way to *make* it a surprise was to convince him that, because of his failure to cooperate, he wasn't going to get it.

The whole business put me into a somewhat surly mood. And my temper wasn't improved any when I was at my office one day, and the telephone rang. It was Teddy completing his first call! He was mighty excited, because he had never dialed a number successfully before.

"Hello, Daddy," he crowed. "Mama showed me how, and now I can call you all the time. Isn't that splendid? You and I can have some good, long talks even when you're at the office, eh Dad?"

"Oh, great," I responded.

"I know all the holes to put my fingers in," he explained.

"Peachy," I said. "Now let me talk to Mama."

I figured Mary would be hovering over him, proud of his achievement, and she was. I guess she had been sharing the receiver, because she came on the line immediately.

"What hath you wrought?" I rebuked her. "I'll *never* manage to get any work done from now on."

"I only had to show him twice," she boasted, "and after that he could do it all by himself. Only four years old, and he can use the telephone!"

"Since he can't read letters or numbers, how does he do it?" I couldn't refrain from asking.

"He just *remembers*," she explained. "He must have a photographic memory."

"If you're so good at teaching him, I wish you'd teach him how to tell time."

"No, that's your department. By the way, what *are* you going to do about that electric train. Surely, the grim disciplinarian of the family isn't going to back down and . . ."

"I'm going to do just what you'd do," I interrupted, "and you know it."

Teddy came back on the phone then, and he and I talked some more. And then, after we hung up, he called again, just to keep his hand in. Then he called a third time, to prove that the first two calls weren't flukes—like the million monkeys pounding on typewriter keys for a million years and finally coming up with Shakespeare's complete works. I certainly wished that Mary had taught him some other telephone number, like her mother's house or the Salvation Army, instead of mine.

And then I got the idea that let me off the hook.

CHAPTER 16

ELECTRIC TRAINS

IF YOU CAN BELIEVE MOST OF THE WITTY ESSAYS THAT HAVE
been written about electric trains, fathers always monopolize
them. Daddy starts to hog the train on Christmas morning,
and Junior doesn't even get a smell of it until Valentine's
Day or later.

The fathers in those essays are probably Young Marrieds
—the same sort of enthusiastic citizens who like to preside
over cook-outs, to perform do-it-yourself projects in the

147

patio, and to drive sporty convertibles with the tops down.

I hope that I will not picture myself as an aging spoilsport when I report here that I have just about outgrown electric trains. The same goes for charcoal grills, patios, and convertibles—all of which involve more sun, dust, and insects than I enjoy.

Actually, I think that life was simpler when toys—both for children and adults—were simpler. I rate expensive mechanical toys right along with TV sets as something deliberately designed to add to a man's tensions. Even after everyone in the house is sick-to-death of expensive toys you still feel duty bound to play with them, as a matter of simple economy.

When I was a boy some children *ten* or *twelve* years old had electric trains. But a piece of string attached to a little wooden elephant, mounted on four wooden wheels, was considered a perfectly adequate toy for a four-year-old. A child Teddy's age ran around the house pulling one end of the string, and the elephant followed—and that was that! If the string broke, the father could tie a knot in it; if one of the wheels came off, he could put it back on again with a nail and a hammer.

I don't believe that anyone makes plain wooden elephants any more, and most four-year-olds would think it was an imposition to have to propel their own toys.

The last toy elephant I've seen was one Teddy received that Christmas. It ran by batteries—under a remote-control arrangement which allowed the child to loll in a chair while pressing buttons—and blew soap bubbles through its trunk.

Even so, this mechanized elephant was overshadowed by the electric train, which came in a corrugated box as big as a suitcase. I gave the train to Teddy right after he had worn out the elephant's batteries, and he was mighty pleased with it, all right. Mary and his nurse, exchanging happy glances over each of his facial expressions, crowded around as he opened the carton.

Despite the happy glances, they remarked all but simultaneously, just as Teddy picked up his new engine, that *they* had thought I wasn't going to give him an electric train unless he could tell time.

I had anticipated this negative attitude. And it was my cue to execute the bright idea I had had a few weeks before, when Teddy had telephoned me at the office.

"You are a hundred-per-cent correct," I replied. "He can tell time right now."

"Go along!" said his nurse.

"You know very well he can't," said Mary. "I tested him just last night, to see whether you'd make your deadline. And he didn't show any progress at all."

"If I ask him what time it is and he tells me," I inquired, "isn't that telling time?"

They had to admit it was.

"Teddy," I asked, falling casually into his customary inversion, "what time it is?"

"What time it is?" he repeated just as casually. "Did you say 'what time it is?' "

"Yes indeed I did," I said. He and I had been rehearsing this for several days, and we couldn't resist hamming it up a little.

"Just a second, Daddy," he replied nonchalantly, "and I shall go see."

"Please do," I said.

"I'll be happy to."

He walked across the room to the telephone, and started to dial.

"That's cheating, Mr. Gilbreth," the nurse admonished me.

"It certainly is," Mary agreed indignantly. "He's dialing the Time of Day Service, isn't he?"

"Suppose he is?" I catechized. "Who made up the conditions for this electric train anyway, you or me? When I tell him he has to do something to earn a reward, I stick to my guns, believe me."

"Like fun!" protested the nurse.

"*Sure* you do!" added Mary.

Teddy, having finished dialing, listened intently. Then he hung up the telephone and rejoined our group. He looked for all the world like the cat who had swallowed the canary.

"Did you ask me what time it is, Daddy?" he inquired.

"I did, indeed."

"Well," he crowed, "it is exactly . . ." His face fell, and

he stamped the floor in frustration. "Hells bells," he shouted at the top of his voice, "I done forget!"

Mary and his nurse both burst out laughing. But I was mad that the trick hadn't worked, and so I took it out on him for using a forbidden word.

"Blast it all," I told him, "the next time I hear you say 'hells bells' around here . . ."

"That's what *you* say when you're mad," he interrupted.

"I don't care *what* I say. *You're* not allowed to say it. And the next time you do, I'm going to take away your electric train, and . . ."

I stopped lamely. There wasn't any use in being a bad sport, just because I was disappointed. And I certainly ought to have learned by now not to make any threats or promises involving electric trains.

"All I said was what you said," Teddy choked, almost in tears.

"I'm sorry, pal," I apologized. "I'll try not to say it any more. And you'll have to try, too."

"Okay," he managed, and the tears were streaming down his face.

"Do you want to try the time trick again?"

"I guess so."

"It will be almost as good a trick as the first time," I assured him.

"It will?" he brightened a little.

"Of course it will, dear," Mary told him.

"All right then." He was trying to smile.

"Teddy," I asked, "what time it is?"

"What time it is? Did you say 'what time it is?' "

"Yes."

"Just a second, Daddy, and I shall go see."

"Please do."

"I'll be happy to."

He went to the telephone, dialed, listened, and came racing back to us.

"Keep well, keep well the pleasant way, eat Miller's bread *four* times a day," he said pompously. "The time now: ten fifty-two."

Like most young boys today, Teddy is mechanically minded. He takes for granted such things as radar, weightlessness, rockets, and H-bombs, when he encounters them on TV. Children seem to absorb through osmosis both an understanding and a tolerance of the wondrous horrors of their age.

Nevertheless, a four-year-old, however versed in scientific miracles, cannot set up an electric train without some guidance. So I was dragooned on the spot into helping him. Even before I had my second cup of coffee or had examined a single present of my own, I found myself engaged in laying tracks, reading electrical diagrams, hooking up a transformer, erecting scaffolding, locating a station, and goodness knows how many other nice problems of electric, mechanical, and railroad engineering.

Electric-train tracks haven't improved any in the last two-score years. Metal prongs still extend from one end of a segment of track, and these have to be fitted simultaneously into little holes at the opposite end of another segment. Once they are fitted, you push the segments together. It is not as simple as it sounds, though, because usually one of the prongs will pop out at the last minute, and then if you are pushing too hard the prongs will jam painfully into your fingers.

All in all, it is a task for sharp eyes and steady hands, characteristics possessed by four-year-olds in superabundance. Regretfully, I can no longer claim an abundance of either—especially early on Christmas morning.

Also, bifocal glasses and electric railroad tracks do not mix. If you get your head down far enough to use the bottom of the bifocals, your chin is on the floor, your head is bent back until your neck cords become knotted, and your nose bumps the cross-ties. If you try to back off and use the upper part, you get so far way from your work that you can't find the little holes.

Teddy quickly gained the know-how about assembling the tracks and, as already mentioned, he had the eyes and the nerves for the job. Unfortunately, he lacked the physical strength to push the tracks together, once he got the prongs lined up. I tried working with him, applying the pressure after he had done the precision part of the job. But that failed, too, because four hands are just too many for such a delicate task.

So we both became exasperated and lost our tempers and Teddy kept saying:

"Let me do it," "I can do it," "Let me show you," and "Look at *me!*" For my part, I kept demanding that he get his sticky, candy-caned hands out of the way, and his head out of the light.

Both of us were rather completely annoyed with each other, and Christmas spirit was at a minimum, when the last pieces of track were finally joined together. Incidentally, the last junction—the figurative golden spike—is a particularly difficult one, because you are dealing with an oval which threatens to explode into the sum of its individual parts, as you bring the ends together.

By then the coffee was cold and my knees were so stiff I had to use a chair to get on my feet. I leaned over one more time, to help Teddy put the train on the track. You still have to be careful to get the engine's wheels just right, or they will short-circuit the tracks, and shoot out sparks.

"That ought to be it," I said grumpily. "Throw the switch on the transformer, and she should run."

"Or maybe she will blow a fuse, eh Daddy?" he suggested.

"If she does," I said between locked teeth "I am going to see whether any of my presents will gurgle when shaken."

He threw the switch, the transformer hummed, and the

train started moving.

And maybe it was worth all the trouble—well, *some* of the trouble, anyway—as I watched the sheer delight on Teddy's face. Then, as the engine started puffing fake smoke and the train tooled around the track, he piped in a shrill soprano:

"Choo, choo, choo," "All aboard," "Got to stop now for Saluda station," "Tickets, please," "Carry your bag, mister?" and (an anachronism the source of which is not altogether clear) "Whoa there, Nellie."

After awhile, he came over to where I was sitting, still trying to flex my knees, and both of us decided to make up and be friends again.

"We did a pretty good job," he said. "She runs fine, eh Dad?"

"Man, I'll say," I agreed.

"She runs *splendid!* Do you want me to find out what time it is, Daddy?"

"That would be a good idea."

"Any time you want to know the time, Daddy, just ask me."

"I sure will."

He started toward the telephone.

"Don't you want to turn off the train, when you're not playing with it?" I suggested.

"Oh, let her run," he said. "I think she needs the exercise."

CHAPTER 17

THE SHYSTER

WHENEVER ADULTS CAN'T THINK OF ANYTHING SENSIBLE TO say to a boy, they invariably ask him what he wants to be when he grows up. By the time Teddy was almost five years old, he was being asked that question with increasing frequency. His answer was usually, "I don't know" or, "A man."

Sometimes the interrogators, not content to let a sleeping dog lie, would then turn to me and inquire whether he had

157

shown a talent for any particular kind of business. I'd usually reply that he was still a little young for that. The answer wasn't strictly the truth, but how is a father to explain that his son has all the necessary qualifications for a wonderful shyster lawyer?

No criticism of Teddy is intended, though, because I've always had a certain amount of admiration for shysters. In an otherwise self-important profession which has a narcissistic affection for its own dignity and ethics, the shyster is a refreshing scamp who has neither. Yet, feisty as a gun fighter, he has the nerve to battle against overwhelming odds, relying only on his shady acumen in a one-sided duel with the Due Process of Law.

And more often than not, firing a stream of outrageous questions and bald-faced lies, the shyster manages to rout the opposition, confuse the judge, enchant the jury, and win the case.

Teddy did that, all right!

Maybe his shyster stage was partly psychological, caused by the forthcoming addition to our family. But whatever the reason, he emerged that winter as a ruthless cross-questioner and a "storyteller"—as Southerners tactfully label their youthful liars—of munchausenian proportions.

I've already mentioned his "story" about rat poison at Nantucket, and his subsequent stealth about candy. By midwinter, those harbingers had blossomed into all-around shocking shysterism.

When it came to horrid questions, delivered at dead-waking volume, Teddy wrote the manual. I sometimes think I could make a pretty fair living just sending three or four of them a day to those newspapers which offer cash prizes for embarrassing moments. I will list but a few sickening examples:

—"Why does the minister have nothing but freckled skin on the top of his head?"

—"Look at the stuff like snowflakes on the shoulders of that man's blue suit."

—"Why does that lady have such a big, fat stomach? Do you think there is a little baby in there?"

—"Did you know that that lady with the wrinkles can take her teeth right out of her head and wash them in the sink? I *saw* her do it."

My father used to allege that adults should stop what they were doing, and patiently answer every question asked by a child, no matter how trivial or horrid. By adults he meant, of course, all adults but himself.

I'd surely like to know how my father would have answered some of *those!*

"If a child asks 'why,' " he used to say, "the worst answer in the world is 'We don't talk about things like that.' Children have inquiring minds. When they ask a question, they seek to learn a lesson."

As I grew older, I found that he was right about a number of things. But he was entirely wrong about this one.

For the truth is that children ask questions not to learn a lesson, but to teach one.

An almost infinite number of personal interviews with Teddy has led me to conclude that children's questions are designed primarily to discipline parents by irritating and boring them to the point where they will beat a pusillanimous retreat.

To substantiate this thesis, I will reproduce practically verbatim an excerpt from the nightly transcript at my house, with the aforementioned shyster in the pajamaed role of attorney for the defense, trying to prove that he shouldn't be sent to bed.

Q. "Why do I have to go to bed?"

A. "You know why. Because it's seven-thirty."

Q. "What?"

A. "Because it's seven-thirty."

Q. "What?"

A. "I wish you'd stop saying, 'What?' "

Q. "Why?"

A. "Botheration, boy. Because it is repetitious, and annoying, and it indicates that you are not paying attention."

Q. "What's all that mean, for mercy sake?"

A. "Never mind what it means. It means it's time to go to bed."

Q. "Well, why is it my bed time?"

A. "Because it's seven-thirty."

Q. "When I get to be five years old, can I stay up later

than that?"

A. "You'll have to ask your mother."

Q. "When will I be five years old?"

A. "Pretty soon. Now get in that bed."

Q. "Will I be five years old before the new baby comes?"

A. "Ye Gads, no! I hope not."

Q. "And will you get me a cat like you promised?"

A. "If you are good and go to bed."

Q. "When will the new baby have to go to bed?"

A. "New babies *stay* in bed."

Q. "Well, why do you want to treat me like a new baby and make me stay in bed?"

A. "What do you mean, *stay* in bed! You've been up all day."

Q. "Well, I took a good nap this afternoon, didn't I?"

A. "No, you certainly didn't."

Q. "You don't want me to get in bed when my nose is all stopped up, do you?"

A. "Your nose isn't all stopped up. That was two weeks ago, and the doctor fixed you up with some antihistamine."

Q. "You mean Dr. Rooster?"

A. "Okay."

Q. "Dr. Rooster, eh Daddy?"

A. "Yes. That's a funny one. Now get into bed."

Q. "Ho-ho-ho, eh Daddy?"

A. "Sure. Now get into bed."

Q. "What time did you say it was?"

A. "Well, *now* it's twenty-five of eight?"

Q. "Whaaat?"

A. "That's right. You've stalled around for five whole minutes."

Q. "How do you know it's twenty-five of eight?"

A. "Blast it all! Because my watch says so, that's how!"

Q. "Where is your watch?"

A. "Right here on my wrist."

Q. "Well, how do you know it says twenty-five of eight?"

A. "Because the big hand is pointing at thirty-five, and the little hand is coming up to eight."

Q. "But you said twenty-five, not thirty-five, didn't you?"

A. "Yes, but when it says thirty-five after it's really twenty-five of."

Q. "Is it?"

A. "Yes."

Q. "Are you *sure?*"

A. "Dammit it all, boy, *get in that bed!*"

Q. "Did you say 'dammit'?"

A. "Yes, dammit, I said dammit."

Q. "Is that a nice way to talk?"

A. "I guess not."

Q. "Did you say it was thirty-five of eight?"

A. "I said it was twenty-five of eight. But now it's twenty-two of eight."

Q. "Whaaat?"

A. "Exactly."

Q. "Are you sure your watch hasn't stopped? Shall I check it on the telephone?"

A. "No. And of course I'm sure."

Q. "Why are you so sure, Daddy?"

A. "Because the hands are moving, and I can hear it tick."

Q. "Can I hear it tick?"

A. "All right. You can if you'll go right to bed."

Q. "Why?"

Etc.

While I am quoting verbatim, I also may as well list some of his ingenious alibis which are no less than utter falsehoods. Some of the best involve his playpen—or at any rate his *former* playpen.

I've mentioned milestones, on several occasions. The most important milestone of all in the life of a young child occurs not when he learns to walk or talk, but when he learns to climb.

Teddy had learned to climb just before his third birthday. And that meant emancipation. Once a child can get out of a playpen, he becomes his own boss. From that day forward, neither leg irons nor handcuffs can stay him from the swift completion of his unappointed rounds.

Teddy's ability to scale the walls had rendered the playpen obsolete. However, Mary and I were reluctant to scrap it, for a number of reasons—not the least of which was the knowledge that another baby would some day be ripe for incarceration therein.

Another reason was that the vacated playpen served a useful purpose as a well-ventilated depository for miscellaneous treasures, now mostly rusty and broken, which had been showered extravagantly on Teddy since a few months before he was born.

Predominating in this unsanitary trove were enough sticky, food-caked, stuffed and partially stuffed animals to fill a glue factory or a pretty good-sized zoo for the grotesquely handicapped. Almost every specimen looked as if it had weathered a famine, because of Teddy's one-time penchant for removing portions of the stuffing. And *every* specimen was blind, because Mary believed that if the eyes weren't removed, he'd be sure to swallow them. In addition to the starved and the blind, there was also a pretty fair number of lames and halts.

Aside from the animal kingdom, other items included airplanes which couldn't fly on one wing, a collection of discordant musical and percussion instruments, spheres ranging in size from marbles to beach balls, and assorted pieces of jigsaw puzzles, building blocks, modeling clay, crayons, mechanical sets, and other odoriferous objects too numerous or revolting to mention.

Teddy had a deep-seated and amply justified suspicion that Mary and I would like to jettison some of this flotsam from a spoiled infancy. We had tried several times to sneak some of the broken toys into the trash, but he always spotted their absence immediately, and went rummaging into garbage pails. So the easiest thing to do was to stack everything in the playpen.

When we started to do this, Teddy's attitude toward the pen underwent a reversal.

At first you couldn't keep him *in* stir, and then you couldn't keep him out of it. He became so adept at climbing back into his erstwhile cell that he'd scale the walls with a vault, literally knocking the stuffing out of a few more of his wretched animals.

There wouldn't have been any real harm in that, if he hadn't also developed the habit of taking inventory. Standing inside the playpen, he'd go systematically through the pile, throwing the debris piece by piece into every corner of the room. Not until the last lump of modeling clay had bounced moistly off a far wall was he content to climb from the playpen and wend a tortuous path through the noisome wreckage to the hall door.

This sort of shambles may be allowed, if not actually encouraged, by the permissive school of child psychologists. My initial reaction was to tolerate it patiently, provided the perpetrator agreed to pick up the mare's nest within a reasonable time span—say about eighteen seconds.

To date, however, the picking up has taken considerably longer than that. And if the job were left for Teddy to do singlehandedly, without the incentive of an occasional spank, I would estimate that the time span would be closer to eighteen light years than eighteen seconds.

Here, then, is the shyster's summation of why, having dispersed a whole playpen full of miscellanea in a matter of moments, it is utterly impossible for him to put the items *back* in the playpen in a matter of eons:

—He is too exhausted.

—His foot is asleep.

—He has to go to the bathroom, but will see me later, alligator.

—He has awful stomach cramps.

—His nose is all stopped up.

—He doesn't want to strain his muscles.

—It might make him late for work.

—His teacher told him not to.

—He has a loose tooth.

—The Lord told him that's where the poor animals *like* to be.

—He must leave hurriedly, because he forgot (a) to brush his teeth or (b) say his prayers.

—His pants are too darned tight.

—He dassent lean over because of his aching back.

I know all about sparing the rod and spoiling the child. I am also well aware that once you let a child get away with murder, he has your number forever after.

Just the same, I've seen too many examples of parents who, unknowingly, interfered with the proper development of talented children. So I'm not going to have anything like that on my conscience. I don't want to be responsible for inhibiting a child prodigy in the slippery art of cross-questioning, alibiing, and evading.

Anyway, I suppose it goes without saying that the gaffer who is finally saddled with picking up the nursery debris is the poor old rod-sparer whose pants really *are* too darned tight, who actually possesses an aching back, and who *certainly* is going to be late for work.

CHAPTER 18

REBECCA

WE NAMED THE BABY REBECCA MOTTE, AFTER A CHARLES-
ton woman whose cool dignity helped keep the British in
line during the Revolution. The first Rebecca's house still
stands on King Street, not far from the Battery. Sir Henry
Clinton, the British commander, and his staff took over the
house as their general headquarters. In fact a caricature of
the general, scratched with a diamond and bearing his name,

can still be seen in a marble mantelpiece there. Sir Henry insisted that Mrs. Motte continue to preside over the dinner table, with himself and his officers as "guests." And she did so—day after day—but never failed first to lock her three highly nubile daughters in the garret. Subsequently, the British also occupied her plantation house, near what is now Columbia, and converted it into a fort. Light-Horse Harry Lee reluctantly informed Mrs. Motte that he might have to burn down the plantation house, and her reply became a rallying cry in South Carolina:

"Do not hesitate a minute."

I couldn't take Teddy to the hospital to see his mother and new sister, because children his age weren't allowed. But I tried to condition him for the day Rebecca would be brought home.

"Your new sister," I told him, "is a little bit of a thing— not much bigger than *that*."

"That's not very big," he agreed cautiously. "I'm *much* bigger than that, eh Daddy?"

"You surely are. And since you're bigger, you're going to have to be sure to act like an older brother, and help us take care of her. From now on, you have responsibilities. And when a person has responsibilities, he's important."

"Am I important enough to have my own cat like you promised?" he asked.

"You surely are. I'm going to get you a cat the day Rebecca comes home. How do you like her name?"

"Her name's Lila," he said.

"No it isn't. It's Rebecca."

"I'm not talking about *her*. Why do we have to talk about *her* all day long? I'm talking about my cat."

"What about your cat?"

"Her name's Lila."

"That's a nice name. Where did you get it? Why Lila?"

"Why Rebecca?" he asked.

The conversation reminded me vaguely of naming *The Strawberry*.

"Anyway, she's awfully cute," I said. "She wants to eat all the time, and she has hardly any hair, and I think her eyes are blue."

"Go along," he scoffed. "Whoever heard of a blue-eyed cat with hardly no hair, eh Daddy?"

"I'm talking about . . ."

"Rebecca," he finished for me, with a sigh. "Why do you always want to talk about her?"

Before Mary went to the hospital, she had made an appointment for Teddy to get a tetanus shot, and I fell heir to the chore of taking him to the doctor's. Although I had accompanied Mary on many such trips, I had never had to handle it all by myself before. So I called the doctor, for a helping hand.

"Give me a break," I urged him, "and don't keep me out there in the waiting room with all those mothers and children, while Ted fusses. I'll tell him I'm taking him to get an ice-cream cone, see? Then we'll just happen to pass your office, and I'll jam on the brakes, grab him, and . . ."

"He's almost five years old, and you've got to stop treating him like a baby," the doctor scolded me. "Put him on the phone, and I want you to listen to what I tell him."

"If you scare him," I threatened, "I'm not bringing him, that's all. You can just cart your needle out here and run him down by yourself. I won't even help you pin him to the floor."

"Put him on, will you?" he asked impatiently. "I've got a whole office full of sick children waiting for me."

"Bid deal," I grumbled.

But I explained to Teddy who it was, and then we both listened at the receiver.

"Hi, Ted," said the Doctor. "Do you know who this is?"

"Dr. Rooster," Ted acknowledged none too enthusiastically.

"I hear you're a big brother now."

"You do?"

"I certainly do."

"So do I."

"Fine. Well older brothers can't be cry babies any more. So I want you to come down here with your mentally retarded old daddy and get a tetanus shot, you hear me?"

"I guess so."

"If you come right now, I won't keep you waiting."

"All right."

"And, listen, Teddy . . ."

"What?"

"I don't want you to cry, either. You're too old for that now. And older brothers aren't supposed to cry about tetanus shots."

Teddy didn't say anything to that, and finally the doctor asked:

"Did you hear me, Ted?"

"Yes."

"All right, then. Are you going to act like an older brother, or are you going to cry? And are you going to hold your arm out for me, or is your daddy going to have to wrestle with you?"

"I'll *try* to act like an older brother," said Ted.

"Good Boy!" the doctor and I said simultaneously.

"And I'll hold out my arm," he promised. "And if I cry, I think I'll only cry a little bit."

As it turned out, he didn't cry at all.

There's a golden glow when a man carries a new baby into his house, with his wife holding protectively to his arm.

In the bossy atmosphere of the hospital, he hasn't even been able to touch his child—to run the back of his fingers over the gossamer silkiness of her skin, or to tickle the tiny feet to make her smile.

But now, with the little thing stirring in his arms, the full impact of the miracle strikes home.

Because, while science knows more than it needs to know about how to wipe out human lives, it still takes an individual man and a woman to create one. And the new life has instantly become all important in the scheme of things. Why the baby has already changed the statistics of the world! And that alone is quite an accomplishment for such a little creature, when you stop to think about it.

More than that, the baby represents living proof of immortality, a wondrous privilege denied to some. If all of this sounds weighty, there is a gay side, too. For the fact is that nothing can brighten-the-corner-where-you-are like the sunshine of a new baby. You can't beat a baby as a conversation piece or as something to cuddle. Her cooing is the happiest sound in the world, and the righteous self-pity of her caterwauling, when she imagines herself to be abused, can be one of the most comical. To succor such a helpless little creature—who grows every day to look more like a human being, if not like yourself—is one of the few completely self-satisfying experiences in a man's lifetime. And I feel sorry for anyone who has deliberately passed it up.

We entered the front door, and Teddy came seat-first down the banisters to meet us. Mary hadn't seen him for almost a week, so of course she had to greet him, even before he was allowed to look at the baby. She kissed him, down where his neck meets his shoulders, which always causes him to giggle, pull in his head like a turtle, and holler, "Quit that!" Just the same, you could tell he liked it.

"Well, what do you think of your little sister?" I finally asked him noncommittally, trying to walk the tightrope between an old flame and a new love.

"Let me have a good look at her," he replied.

I leaned over and held Rebecca down where he could see her. Teddy blinked, and his mouth dropped open. I don't think he had expected her to be so small or to have that pinched-up face of all new babies. But he didn't answer until he had full control of himself.

"Why," he exclaimed in such artificial tones that it sounded as if he had been eavesdropping at a bridal shower, "isn't that *simply* darling!"

I couldn't help snickering, but Mary preferred to accept the remark at face value.

"What a nice thing to say!" she told him. "And you're going to be good to your little sister, aren't you, Teddy?"

"I *think* so," he replied, using a somewhat more candid tone of voice. "Why did you want to stay in the hospital so long for?"

"I didn't exactly want to," Mary explained. "The doctor made me."

"Doctor Rooster?"

"No, my doctor."

"And did your doctor give you a shot?"

"Gracious," she stooged for him, "*did* he!"

"And did that little baby have a shot?"

"She certainly did."

"Did that little baby cry?"

"She almost cried her eyes out!"

Far from distressing Teddy, that bit of news seemed to please him inordinately.

"Little babies are cry babies, eh Daddy?" he asked me. "I didn't cry at all when I had my shot while Mama was in the hospital, did I, Daddy?"

"That's right," I confirmed.

"And from now on," he continued optimistically, "I'm not *never* going to cry no more. Even when Daddy takes out splinters!"

"My, what a big boy!" Mary praised him.

It seemed to me that everything was proceeding pretty well, and that so far we had played our cards just right.

Teddy's nurse came in then—only now she was going to be Rebecca's nurse. She, too, realized the necessity for tact.

"My, what a lovely baby," she said, also trying to keep her voice noncommittal. "Don't you think Rebecca is lovely, Teddy?"

"*Simply* darling," he repeated.

I handed her the baby, and that was more than Teddy could tolerate. He knew he couldn't order Mary and me around, but he had no intention of letting his nurse divide her affections.

"You put that baby down!" he ordered, stamping his feet.

"Why, *Teddy!*" she protested. "That's no way to talk to me."

"That's Mama's baby, not yours," he shouted, almost in tears. "Let *her* hold the baby!"

"Come on, Teddy Boy," the nurse jollied him, "let's take your little sister upstairs, and put her in the crib."

"In *my* crib?" he roared. "You're going to give her *my* crib?"

"Look here," I interceded, "you haven't slept in that crib for months. That's Rebecca's crib now, not yours."

"Whaaat?" he whinnied.

"I explained all that to you yesterday, when we brought the crib down from the attic," I said.

"Maybe you explained it," he choked, and now his eyes were brimming with tears, "but you didn't put no baby in it. That's *my* crib. It don't *belong* to her."

"But you'll lend it to her, won't you?" Mary asked. "You'll be generous to your little sister, won't you?"

"Why does she want to sleep here all the time?" he dodged the questions.

"Because she lives *here*, that's why," I said, beginning to lose patience.

"Whaaat!"

"Listen, I *told* you she was coming here to stay."

"But you didn't tell me she was going to *sleep* here, and that *my nurse* was going to pat her like that!"

"You have to pat little babies," the nurse explained.

"I vote we take her back to the hospital," Teddy decided.

Almost as if she had heard him, Rebecca opened her eyes, looked at him, and started to bawl.

"Ye gads and little dishes," sighed Teddy, who apparently thought that was the straw which broke the camel's back. "All right, cry-baby-crispy. You can have my crib, then!"

Rebecca kept crying, and Teddy began to feel contrite.

"If you keep quiet," he promised her after awhile, "I'll let you play with my new cat, whose name is . . . Hey, Dad!" he suddenly remembered. "Mercy sakes! Where is my cat? You *promised* that when you brought the baby home, I could have a kitty."

"We'll get the cat in a few minutes," I assured him. "She's all picked out and waiting for us, over at your uncle's house."

"Let's go get her then," he urged, and all the tears were gone now. "Come on."

"All right," I agreed. Frankly, Rebecca's crying was beginning to get on my nerves, too.

"Teddy, would you like to hold the baby for a minute before you go?" Mary asked gently.

He thought it over. And I guess he decided that, after being so selfish about his crib, holding Rebecca was the least he could do.

"Oh, all right," said the little martyr. "Give her to me, then."

I sat him down in a rocker, and the nurse put Rebecca in

his lap. The baby was still caterwauling. But as Teddy started
to rock, she quieted down. Then, all of a sudden, she opened
her eyes and gave him a slow, wet-eyed smile.

"Gracious peace!" he whispered in awe, still rocking
slowly. "She's decided to shut up. And I believe she *likes*
me." Rebecca smiled at him again. This time he smiled back.
"She's *crazy* about me!" he announced with typical modesty.

I looked at the two of them rocking there, and all of a
sudden I felt as if I had to swallow hard. He needs a haircut, I told myself, as if it were his fault. As *usual*, he needs
a haircut. And who was it said that all new babies look just
like Churchill—she's a ringer for Winnie, all right. Why
won't that boy learn to keep the heels of those cowboy boots
the hell off the furniture. I guess if I've told him once, I've
told him a thousand times.

"All right, Boy Friend," I finally said. "Come on, then,
if you want to get your cat. I've got to get back to work *some-
time* today."

"Not right now," he said. "I'm too busy right now."

"Don't you want to get your cat?"

"Maybe so. But *first* I want to rock my baby sister."

"But the cat's waiting for us," I insisted. "And I've got to
get back to work."

"You go ahead back to work, then."

"Don't you want to get your cat?"

"Why," he complained, "does everyone want to talk about
a cat all day?"